Fodor's
25 Best

MILAN

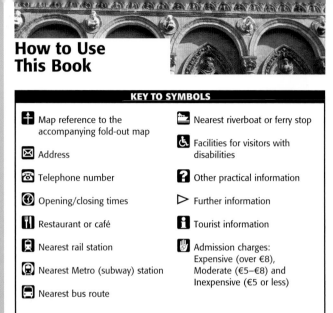

How to Use This Book

KEY TO SYMBOLS

✛ Map reference to the accompanying fold-out map

✉ Address

☎ Telephone number

🕐 Opening/closing times

🍴 Restaurant or café

🚆 Nearest rail station

Ⓜ Nearest Metro (subway) station

🚌 Nearest bus route

🛳 Nearest riverboat or ferry stop

♿ Facilities for visitors with disabilities

❓ Other practical information

▷ Further information

ℹ Tourist information

✋ Admission charges: Expensive (over €8), Moderate (€5–€8) and Inexpensive (€5 or less)

This guide is divided into four sections

● Essential Milan: An introduction to the city and tips on making the most of your stay.

● Milan by Area: We've broken the city into five areas, and recommended the best sights, shops, entertainment venues, nightlife and where to eat in each one. Suggested walks help you to explore on foot.

● Where to Stay: The best hotels, whether you're looking for luxury, budget or something in between.

● Need to Know: The info you need to make your trip run smoothly, including getting about by public transport, weather tips, emergency phone numbers and useful websites.

Navigation In the Milan by Area chapter, we've given each area its own color, which is also used on the locator maps throughout the book and the map on the inside front cover.

Maps The fold-out map with this book is a comprehensive street plan of Milan. The grid on this fold-out map is the same as the grid on the locator maps within the book. We've given grid references within the book for each sight and listing.

Contents

CONTENTS

Introducing Milan

There's an old adage, *"Milan l'è Milan"*—Milan is just Milan. The city may seem to lack the charm of other Italian cities, but if you scratch beneath the surface you will find this is a city of contrasts and hidden depths, with its own unique personality.

Milan's reputation is one of commercialism driven by market forces, and indeed it is the power-house of Italy's economy. But this city is not just about commercial-ism. Despite a distinctly more northern European attitude to business and a commitment to an up-to-the-minute lifestyle, the traditional Italian way of life has not been totally rejected.

This is a stylish city, whose inhab-itants are used to good design, quality and flair across the board. It has some of the finest churches in Italy and many *palazzi*, proud reminders of the city's aristocratic past. The many well-run museums offer a glimpse into the city's artis-tic and historic heritage. There is fantastic shopping, from chic designer stores to street markets.

Just beyond the *centro storico* there are other districts with a totally different feel, like the Navigli, where renovation has rejuvenated the area. You will also discover pretty parks and hidden gardens that act as tranquil oases from the hustle and bustle.

While it does have a lot of traffic and rush-hour congestion, the city is a comfortable place to live and exudes a sense of well-being— and, unlike some other Italian cities, the Milanese don't make excessive use of their car horns. Public transportation is excellent: efficient, clean and reasonably priced. The Milanese are happy in their own skin, unruffled and confi-dent—busy, yes, but they always find time to be sociable.

Milan may not have the beauty of Florence, the grandeur of Rome or the romance of Venice, but it does have something very appealing all of its own.

FACTS AND FIGURES

- Area of city: 118sq km (45.5sq miles)
- Population: 1.7 million in 2017
- Trade fairs in Milan draw over 4 million visitors per year
- Milan is Italy's largest industrial city, with textiles, car-manufacturing and machinery heading the list
- Over 20 percent of Milan's population is made up of immigrants

MILAN FOR FREE

There are many free museums in Milan and churches do not charge for entry, although there may be a small fee to see a specific painting. Parco Sempione is free to wander but its various attractions may carry a fee. Exploring the canal district and the old artist quarter of Brera or window-shopping in the designer streets won't cost anything either—that's if you can resist.

MILAN'S SKYSCRAPERS

Milan has more than 25 skyscrapers over 100m (328ft) tall, many award-winning and acclaimed as among the world's finest. The Unicredit Tower, designed by César Pelli, tops 231m (758ft) with its spire and is the tallest building in Italy, with Arata Isozaki's Allianz Building (209m/685ft) and Zaha Hadid's twisted Generali Tower (191m/626ft) hot on its heels.

FASHION SHOWS

Milan Fashion Week, held in spring and autumn, is part of the global "Big Four" that includes London, Paris and New York. Italy's top internationally renowned designers, such as Prada, Missoni, Dolce & Gabbana, Versace and Moschino, all showcase their collections here, using venues right across the city. The fashion industry brings millions of euros into the economy.

A Short Stay in Milan

DAY 1

Morning Beat the crowds and start your day around 8.30 at the Pinacoteca di Brera (▷ 29), which has the best art collection in the city.

Mid-morning Just a short walk south is **Teatro alla Scala** (▷ 53); take a peek inside this famous opera house as you pass by. Stroll through **Galleria Vittorio Emanuele II** (▷ 48–49), taking in a few shops along the way. Stop for a coffee break at **Camparino in Galleria** (▷ 59) and watch the world go by while admiring the **Duomo** (▷ 44–45) laid out before you. Visit the Duomo and, on a fine day, scale the 165 steps for an unbeatable city view.

Lunch Seek out one of the tempting eateries in or around Piazza del Duomo; try **Savini** (▷ 60) in the Galleria Vittorio Emanuele II or perhaps **Charleston** (▷ 59) in Piazza del Liberty, or head up Corso Vittorio Emanuele II, where there are several more options.

Afternoon If you continue along Corso Vittorio Emanuele II to Via Montenapoleone and go north, you'll come to the **Quadrilatero d'Oro** (▷ 30–31). Explore this network of pretty streets known as the Golden Quad—Milan's sensational shopping area. In the middle of the afternoon, try to work your way toward **Cova** (▷ 39), where you can rest your weary feet while you have a coffee and mouthwatering cake.

Dinner From the top end of Montenapoleone, it's a short walk west to the **Brera district** (▷ 74). Join in "happy hour" at one of the trendy bars and then have a unique dining experience at **L'Osteria di Brera** (▷ 78).

Evening After dinner wander around the winding medieval streets of this attractive area, soaking up the lively atmosphere.

DAY 2

Morning Reserve tickets well in advance to admire da Vinci's *Last Supper* first thing in the morning at **Santa Maria delle Grazie** (▷ 72–73). If you don't have tickets, check out the beautiful church and its cloisters instead.

Mid-morning Walk a little farther down Corso Magenta to **Biffi** (▷ 78) for a quick pit-stop before heading north to **Parco Sempione** (▷ 70). Enter the park on the west side, pass the Palazzo dell'Arte and for a great view take the elevator to the top of the Torre Branca. Spend some time rambling among the lakes, modern sculptures and monuments.

Lunch There are several cafés in the park where you can have lunch or, if the weather is fine, take a picnic lunch to eat on the grass.

Afternoon Head toward the northeast perimeter of the park and pay a visit to the **Acquario** (▷ 74). Leave this underwater world behind and follow the path round to the clocktower at the front of Castello Sforzesco.

Mid-afternoon Wander down the wide, walkable **Via Dante** (▷ 55), packed with café options for a coffee break. Retrace your steps back to **Castello Sforzesco** (▷ 65) and go inside the massive fortress for a look around. If you have time, visit one of the Castello's interesting museums or relax in the courtyard gardens.

Dinner Take the metro from Cadorna to Porta Genova and walk south to the **Navigli** (▷ 86). Take a stroll along the towpaths on either side of the canal before dining at **Al Pont de Ferr** (▷ 92).

Evening Seek out one of the increasing number of popular nightspots concealed in the side streets of this district.

Top 25

▶ ▶ ▶

Arco della Pace ▷ 64
Triumphal arch in memory of the European peace of 1815.

Teatro alla Scala ▷ 53
One of the world's most famous opera houses, which remains the cultural focus for the city's well-to-do.

Santa Maria presso San Satiro ▷ 52 Bramante-designed church, famed for its painted optical illusion.

Santa Maria delle Grazie ▷ 72–73 Da Vinci's *The Last Supper* is here in the refectory of this significant church.

San Maurizio ▷ 71
The church exterior does not do justice to the superb frescoes displayed inside.

San Lorenzo Maggiore ▷ 87 Early Christian basilica concealing a superb interior and wonderful frescoes.

Quadrilatero d'Oro ▷ 30–31 Enticing shop-window displays at the heart of the fashion industry.

Basilica di Sant' Ambrogio ▷ 82–83 A prototype for Lombardian Romantic-style churches.

Castello Sforzesco ▷ 65
A museum complex housed in an austere and forbidding fortress.

Pinacoteca di Brera
▲ ▷ 29 One of Italy's top galleries, and the focus of most visitors to the Brera.

Pinacoteca Ambrosiana ▷ 51 The oldest art gallery in Milan, founded by Cardinal Federico Borromeo.

Parco Sempione ▷ 70
Gracious parkland unfurls around the Castello Sforzesco.

ESSENTIAL MILAN TOP 25

These pages are a quick guide to the Top 25, which are described in more detail later. Here they are listed alphabetically, and the tinted background shows which area they are in.

Corso Magenta ▷ 66–67 An historic street where the big draw is Leonardo da Vinci's *The Last Supper*.

Duomo ▷ 44–45 The hub of the city and the world's largest Gothic cathedral.

Fondazione Prada ▷ 46–47 Ex-industrial site transformed into a contemporary art space.

Galleria Vittorio Emanuele II ▷ 48–49 A massive arcade known as "the living-room of Milan".

GAM (Galleria d'Arte Moderna) ▷ 24–25 A wonderful neoclassical gallery surrounded with gardens.

Giardini Indro Montanelli ▷ 26 Escape the noise of the city here.

HangarBicocca ▷ 96–97 Ex-aircraft hangar complex now a huge innovative art space.

Museo Bagatti Valsecchi ▷ 27 Works of art and furniture displayed in a Renaissance *palazzo*.

Museo Civico Archeologico ▷ 68–69 The story of Roman Milan told through finds.

Museo Nazionale della Scienza e della Tecnologia ▷ 84–85 Superb technical-science museum.

Museo Poldi Pezzoli ▷ 28 A private art collection of great Italian works.

THE NORTHEAST 21–40

PORTA TENAGLIA

RERA

Pinacoteca di Brera

Orto Botanico

QUADRILATERO D'ORO

Giardini Indro Montanelli

GAM

PORTA MONFORTE

Museo Bagatti Valsecchi

Museo Poldi Pezzoli

Teatro lla Scala

Galleria Vittorio Emanuele II

Duomo

Santa Maria presso San Satiro

Palazzo Reale

Giardino Guastalla

CENTRO STORICO 41–60

Fondazione Prada

Palazzo Reale ▷ 50 The neoclassical Royal Palace, with fine restored rooms, houses several museums.

Navigli ▷ 86 Once a hive of commercial activity and now a gentrified area of shops bars and trattorias.

◀ ◀ ◀

Shopping

Milan is said to be the world's design capital, and a visit to its sensational fashion district is high on many visitors' itineraries, especially as designer clothes can cost less here than in New York or London.

The Golden Quad
Milan's most popular shopping area for *haute couture* is without doubt the network of pretty streets known as the Golden Quad, bordered by Via Montenapoleone, Via Manzoni, Via Sant'Andrea and Via Spiga. Here you will find designer clothes, accessories, shoes and leatherwear presented in chic, minimalist interiors that are works of art themselves. Even when the shops are closed, the streets are full of visitors admiring the window displays.

Other Options
You can also shop for superior goods at the glass-domed Galleria Vittorio Emanuele II (▷ 48); the bohemian Corso di Porta Ticinese, where there are smaller, trendy boutiques; or the up-and-coming Isola area, with some interesting boutiques. There are plenty of less elite stores selling more affordable items around Corso Vittorio Emanuele II, Via Torino, Corsa di Porta Romana and Corso Buenos Aires.

Interior Design Excellence
Milan is also at the forefront of interior design, ranging from the elegant to the wacky. Large

FACTORY OUTLETS
At Milan's factory outlets you can pick up great bargains, with last season's lines from top designers often for sale at a third or less the original price. Many lie outside the city, but all are connected by regular shuttle bus services from the center. Among the best are Serravalle (mcarthurglen. com), with more than 300 top designer stores; Vicolungo (vicolungo.thestyleoutlets.it), 30 minutes out of town; and Scalo Milano (scalomilano.it), 15 minutes out, which has huge discounts on interior decor, home furnishings and fashion, and a great selection of restaurants and cafés.

Shopping is the number one pastime in Milan, be it for the latest designer creation, sun-ripened tomatoes on the

ultramodern showrooms stocked with original trendsetting items are apparent throughout the city. Smaller items that can easily be taken home include kitchen gadgets, decorated glass and sleek, stylish lighting.

Traditional Gifts

If you are looking for more traditionally Milanese products to take home, try some *panettone* (▷ panel below) or pick up a bottle of fine Italian wine from a reputable *enoteca*, where every purchase is beautifully wrapped and you can usually sample before you buy. For that special gift, head to one of the delightful stationery shops that stock hand-crafted paper-based products. The items are produced using luxury paper, handmade from such materials as silk, coconut, lace and bamboo, in every color and shade. They will need to be carefully packed for the journey home.

Antiques Heaven

Antiques enthusiasts will enjoy browsing in the numerous antiques shops around the Brera district and along the canals, where regular antiques markets (▷ 90, panel) are held. Shops specializing in old and new prints and lithographs, art galleries and auction houses are plentiful in Milan. For book lovers, the city has more than its fair share of well-stocked book-shops, some selling books in many languages. There are also smaller, specialist bookshops that stock rare or out-of-print books.

PANETTONE

This famous Milanese cake, made with eggs, flour, sugar, candied fruits and spices, is now served at Christmas throughout Italy. It is said to have originated in the 15th century when the dessert at the Christmas Eve banquet for Ludovico Sforza was burned. It was rescued by Toni, a kitchen boy, who salvaged the remains of the burned cake and added new ingredients. Since that day 'pan del Toni' became known as *panettone* and has remained popular ever since.

vine, delicious cakes and pastries or gadgets and gifts

Shopping by Theme

Whether you're looking for a department store, a quirky boutique, or something in between, you'll find it all in Milan. On this page shops are listed by theme. For a more detailed write-up, see the individual listings in Milan by Area.

ESSENTIAL MILAN   SHOPPING BY THEME

Milan by Night

After-hours entertainment in cosmopolitan Milan is vibrant; the city is known for having Italy's most fashionable nightlife. For the energetic, there are glitzy clubs, bars, disco-pubs, lively cafés and live music venues. If you prefer a slower pace, the city offers world-class opera, ballet and a theater season that is the best and most varied in Italy.

What's Hot

Things don't get going until after dark, when Milan's partygoers come out to play and the streets are thronged with beautiful people. Evenings begin slowly, with the *passeggiata*, where everyone struts up and down the central streets, mainly around Galleria Vittorio Emanuele II and the pedestrian zones along Via Dante. Three popular areas to visit are the Navigli, bisected by waterways and dotted with *osterie* and jazz bars, the atmospheric Brera district, with intimate cafés and restaurants, and the area from Corso Como, through Corso Garibaldi, to the cutting-edge Isola district.

A Little Culture

Opera fans will want to see a performance at La Scala, Milan's famous opera house. The season runs from December to July, but performances sell out fast. There are many other places to enjoy classical music in the city, as well as live theater, cultural events and a wide repertoire of plays. The city's many cinemas often show the new releases ahead of other Italian cities.

Opera and all that jazz—you can find it all in Milan, with great music venues and places just for a drink

---

DISCO-PUBS

Milan has a breed of pub popular with those who want to dance without being plunged into the noise and flashing lights of a full-blown disco; these are known as disco-pubs. Disco-pubs are ideal if you prefer to start the evening with a relaxing drink and quiet conversation, slowly building up to a party mood. Later into the evening the volume is turned up and the pub really starts to swing as every available space is taken up by disco divas performing the latest dance moves.

Where to Eat

The Milanese, like all Italians, love to eat, and the accent lies heavily on regional and seasonal dishes. The city's restaurants reflect both this and the tastes of its international community, resulting in a food scene that combines tradition with imagination.

Meals and Mealtimes

Many working Milanese eat breakfast in a bar (a cappuccino and a sweet pastry). The day starts early, so if you are heading for breakfast in a bar, most open for business around 7–7.30. Hotels usually serve a buffet breakfast complete with fruit juice, cereal, cold meats and cheeses, which normally starts at 8, or earlier in business hotels. Lunch and dinner comprise *antipasto* (starter), *il primo* (pasta, risotto or soup), *secondo* (fish or meat) with *contorni* (vegetables) on the side, and *dolce* (dessert) or cheese. There's no pressure to wade through the whole menu; it's quite acceptable to order just one or two courses.

Where to Eat

Trattorie/osterie are usually family-run, serving simple authentic cooking and open for lunch and in the evening. But nowadays the name *osteria* is being adopted by trendier restaurants (▷ 92, panel). *Ristoranti* are smarter and are not always open for lunch. *Pizzerie* (▷ 59, panel) specialize in pizzas, but often serve simple pasta dishes as well. Some establishments still try to add a cover charge, which includes bread, and a service charge to the bill.

SNACKS

Bars serve hot and cold drinks, alcohol and snacks throughout the day. It's customary to eat or drink standing up; you will pay extra to sit down. Make your request and pay at the cash desk, then take the receipt and go to the bar where you will be served. *Távole calde* are stand-up snack bars that serve freshly prepared hot food. *Gelaterie* (▷ 40, panel) sell a range of ice cream, served in a cone or tub. The best ice cream is made on the premises.

Eat in style—Milan is a great place for dining alfresco, for coffee, lunch or a delectable ice cream

Where to Eat by Cuisine

There are places to eat to suit all tastes and budgets in Milan. On this page they are listed by cuisine. For a more detailed description of each venue, see Milan by Area.

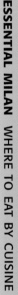

Top Tips For...

These great suggestions will help you tailor your ideal visit to Milan, no matter how you choose to spend your time. Each sight or listing has a fuller write-up elsewhere in the book.

CUTTING-EDGE DESIGN
Cruise the Quadrilatero d'Oro (▷ 30–31), Italy's high spot for fashion, to see window displays presenting designers' creations straight off the catwalk.
Step inside shops like Dolce & Gabbana (▷ 36) on Via della Spiga and be amazed by the innovative interior designs.
Eat at Roberto Cavalli's steel-and-glass restaurant (▷ 78), decked out in his own pioneering designs.

ESCAPING THE HEAT AND NOISE
Lose yourself among the vast lawns and parkland of Parco Sempione (▷ 70).
Take a diversion around the corner from Milan's exclusive shopping area to Giardini Indro Montanelli (▷ 26), where there is something for all interests.
Enjoy the roses in the Parco delle Basiliche (▷ 88), a green oasis linking two great basilicas.
Wander along the towpath of the canals (▷ 86) and find an *osteria* for lunch.

A GOOD NIGHT OUT
La Scala (▷ 58) is a must for a night to remember; book well in advance.
Have a meal and catch a late-night showing at the Cinema Odeon 5 (▷ 58).
Start the evening early by joining happy hour (▷ 91, panel), or with a cocktail at Jamaica (▷ 77) then on to Hollywood (▷ 77) till the early hours.
Join the football-crazy Milanese to see AC or Inter play at the San Siro (▷ 103, panel); discuss the game afterward over a drink at Bar Magenta (▷ 77).

Clockwise from top left: Up-to-the-minute window displays in Milan; plenty of choices on the menus in Milan; stylish eating

A TASTE OF TRADITION

Fraternize with the locals at Trattoria Milanese (▷ 60); nearly a century of tradition is crammed into this homey restaurant, in the heart of the city.

For excellent food that lives up to the Milanese tradition try Solferino (▷ 40), one of Milan's oldest restaurants.

La Latteria (▷ 40) is one of the best examples of good regional cooking in Milan.

YOUR COFFEE IN STYLE

You won't be able to resist Biffi's (▷ 78) mouthwatering chocolate cake.

Cova (▷ 39) is a great place to rest your weary feet from the perils of excessive shopping and just relax.

Enjoy people-watching with your cappuccino at Camparino in Galleria (▷ 59).

THE DOLCE VITA

Join an elite clientele for some luxurious pampering at Principe di Savoia (▷ 112).

Book one of the rooms with chromotherapy, aromatherapy and Japanese massage chaise longues at the Straf (▷ 112).

Indulge yourself in sumptuous surroundings haunted by royals and celebrities at the Grand Hotel et de Milan (▷ 112).

Stay at the opulent Four Seasons hotel (▷ 112) in a 14th-century monastery set around a cloistered courtyard.

TRIPS OUT OF THE CITY

Take a trip well away from the city to beautiful Lake Como, just an hour away by train (▷ 101).

Explore a quintessential Lombard medieval hill town during a visit to Bergamo (▷ 100), in the southern foothills of the Alps.

Head for Cremona to see medieval architecture and the birthplace of the world's greatest violins (▷ 100).

Take a train and a boat to enjoy the breathtaking islands of Lake Maggiore (▷ 102).

is the order of the day; elaborate oriental decoration on the table; Milan's opera house; a stroll in the park

HOME-GROWN DESIGNERS

Visit at least one of Giorgio Armani's stores (▷ 35, panel), scattered throughout the Quadrilatero d'Oro.

There's a Dolce & Gabbana (▷ 36) around every street corner.

Treat yourself at Roberto Cavalli (▷ 37, panel), then flaunt your purchase at Just Cavalli Café (▷ 78).

Spoil your feet after all that walking; Salvatore Ferragamo (▷ 37) has just the thing.

Window shop the best of Milanese high fashion as you stroll the streets of the Quadrilatero d'Oro (▷ 30–31).

FUN WITH THE KIDS

Learn about creatures from under the water at the art nouveau Acquario (▷ 74).

Try the hands-on exhibits at the Science and Technology Museum (▷ 84–85).

Allow the kids to let off steam in Parco Sempione (▷ 70), and then have a picnic.

Sit on swivelling seats and gaze at the stars in the Planetarium (▷ 26).

IF FUNDS ARE SHORT

Visit the city's free museums, which include Museo di Milano (▷ 32–33).

Save up to 25 percent at one of Milan's designer factory outlets (▷ 10, panel).

If you're likely to use public transport, buy a travel card (▷ 118), it's cheaper.

Consider staying at Hotel Due Giardini (▷ 109) for good value for money.

SOMEWHERE TO DANCE

Rub shoulders with celebs at Tocqueville 13 (▷ 77).

The bank vaults come alive at Le Banque (▷ 58).

Drop in on one of Old Fashion Café's (▷ 77) theme nights.

Hit the floor at super-chic Volt (▷ 91) and lose yourself amid the pounding sounds and fabulous lighting.

From top: A stylish designer suit; fun and games at a kids' workshop; take a tram to the Brera and then go dancing

Milan by Area

The Northeast

The northeast reflects the diverse nature of Milan. At its heart are the chic designer shops for which the city is so famous. Alongside are elegant *palazzi*, interesting museums and a tranquil park.

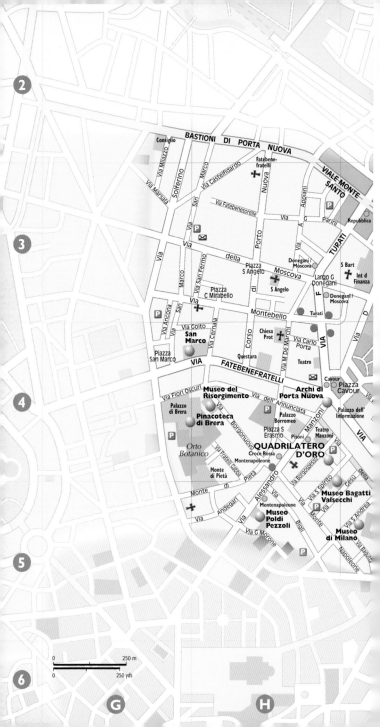

GAM (Galleria d'Arte Moderna)

HIGHLIGHTS

● Marino Marini Collection
● Museo dell'Ottocento
● *Quarto Stato* (Fourth Estate): Pellizza da Volpedo depicts the struggles and sufferings of the working classes
● Lovely wooded gardens

TIP

● Choose a sunny, or at least dry, day to visit the villa and its gardens. You will be close to the Giardini Indro Montanelli for a walk or picnic afterward.

The vast neoclassical Villa Reale has been occupied by Napoleon and Josephine, Count Joseph Radetzky (the Austrian commander-in-chief) and the Italian royal family. Part is now home to the Museo dell'Ottocento (19th-Century Museum).

Famous residents The villa was built in 1790 by Leopold Pollack for Count Ludovico Barbiano di Belgiojoso. After the count's death in the early 19th century, the Italian government donated it as a residence for Napoleon and Josephine, and it passed into the hands of the city of Milan in 1921.

Milanese collectors Occupying 35 rooms, the Museo dell'Ottocento illustrates the main artistic movements of the 19th and early 20th

Il Quarto Stato (The Fourth Estate) *by Guiseppe Pellizza da Polpedo, depicting the workers' march; the painting is displayed in the Museo dell'Ottocento, which is located in the Villa Reale, on the edge of Giardini Indro Montanelli*

century, with emphasis on Italian and French art. The rooms cover art from the neoclassical period to Romanticism, from the Scapigliatura (a Milan-based movement) through Divisionism to Realism. The most important collections are the Grassi, Vismara and Marino. The Marino Marini Collection opened in 1973 and contains bronzes, portrait busts and drawings by the Italian sculptor Marini (1901–80). Some of the busts depict his friends and acquaintances (among them Igor Stravinsky, Henry Miller, Henry Moore and Marc Chagall) and are remarkable for their psychological insight.

Beyond the walls The are good views from the upper floors of the building beside the villa, the Padiglione d'Arte Contemporanea (PAC), which hosts temporary modern art exhibitions.

THE BASICS

gam-milano.com

✚ J4

✉ Via Palestro 16, 20121

☎ 02 8844 5943

🕓 Tue–Sun 9–5.30

🚇 Palestro

🚌 61, 94; tram 1, 2

♿ Good

🎟 Moderate

Giardini Indro Montanelli

TOP
25

Summer rides in the Giardini Indro Montanelli make a welcome change

THE BASICS

➕ J3

✉ Corso Venezia, Via D. Manin, Via Palestro, 20121

🕐 6.30am–dusk

🍴 Café/bar

🚇 Turati, Palestro, Porta Venezia, Repubblica

🚌 61, 94; tram 1, 2, 29, 30

♿ Good

✋ Free

Planetarium

➕ K4

✉ Corso Venezia 57, 20121

☎ 02 8846 3340

🕐 Shows Sep–Jun Tue, Thu 9pm, Sat–Sun 3, 4.30pm; Jul–Aug times vary (see monthly schedule)

🚇 Palestro

🚌 Tram 9, 29, 30

♿ Good

✋ Moderate

HIGHLIGHTS

● Museo di Storia Naturale (▷ 33)
● Planetarium

The largest gardens in Milan were created on the lines of an English park. The attractions and summer entertainment, set among vast greenery and vibrant blooms, are a real breath of fresh air for adults and children alike.

Peace and tranquility The public gardens extend for about 160,000sq m (192,000sq yards). They were enlarged in 1857 by Giuseppe Balzaretto to include the Palazzo Dugnani and the Villa Reale (▷ 24–25). Further changes were made by Emilio Alemagna for the International Expo of 1871, incorporating waterfalls and fountains. Nowadays the gardens provide a welcome escape from the city heat and noise, and attract many joggers and family picnickers. In summer donkey rides, minitrain rides and a merry-go-round keep children amused for hours.

Not just a park There's something here for all ages and interests, from rocks and minerals to bugs. Life-sized crocodiles and snakes seem almost real. On the east side of the park is the Museo di Storia Naturale (▷ 33), popular for its reconstructed dinosaur collection.

View the stars Next to the natural history museum is the Planetario Ulrico Hoepli. The Planetarium, built in 1930, is the biggest in Italy. It has a huge domed room where projections take place. Themes change monthly—call or check details at the tourist office.

Stunning blue-and-white patterned floor at the Museo Bagatti Valsecchi

Museo Bagatti Valsecchi

This museum, in a neo-Renaissance palace, houses fascinating antiques and curios and an extraordinary collection of genuine and reproduction furnishings of the brothers Fausto and Giuseppe Bagatti Valsecchi.

Ardent collectors Fausto and Giuseppe Bagatti Valsecchi, born respectively in 1843 and 1845, inherited their artistic flair from their father, a famous miniaturist. Using a large team of Lombard artisans, they skillfully renovated two *palazzi* (one in Via Gesù, the other backing onto it in Via Santo Spirito) between 1876 and 1895, to be used as their own home. Descendants of the brothers lived here until 1974 and created the Fondazione Bagatti Valsecchi, to open the collection to the public.

Genuine or reproduction? You can visit the brothers' private apartments and the formal rooms they shared: the drawing room, hall of arms, dining room, study and Santo Spirito atrium. The Renaissance setting can be quite convincing—as can be the reproduction furniture that is integrated with the authentic pieces. The Camera Rossa has a display of 15th- to 17th-century children's furniture, and the dining room contains tapestries, sideboards and kitchenware. The library has a number of valuable 15th-century parchments. In the Valtellinese bedroom is a 16th-century bed with carved scenes of *The Road to Calvary* and the Old Testament, and paintings by Giampietrino.

THE NORTHEAST TOP 25

THE BASICS

museobagattivalsecchi.org

⊞ H5

✉ Via Gesù 5, 20121

☎ 02 7600 6132

🕐 Tue–Sun 1–5.45. Usually closed New Year's Day, 6 Jan, Easter, 25 Apr, 1 May, Aug, 1 Nov, 25 Dec, but changes each year

Ⓜ Montenapoleone

🚌 61, 94; tram 1

♿ None

💰 Expensive

ℹ Every room has detailed sheets of information, in six languages. Good guidebook. Audio guides in English

HIGHLIGHTS

● Sala dell'Affresco, named for the fresco by Antonio Boselli of the *Madonna della Misericordia* (1496)
● Library, with painted leather celestial globe
● Valtellinese Bedroom
● The Red Bedroom—Painting of *Santa Giustina de' Borromei*, Giovanni Bellini (c.1475)

Museo Poldi Pezzoli

TOP 25

The Armory (left) and The Gondola on the Lagoon *by Francesco Guardi (right)*

THE BASICS

museopoldipezzoli.it

H5

Via Manzoni 12, 20121

02 794 889

Wed–Mon 10–6. Closed 1 Jan, 6 Jan, Easter, 25 Apr, 1 May, 1 and 15 Aug, 1 Nov, 8 Dec, 25 and 26 Dec

Montenapoleone

61, 94; tram 1, 2

Access to elevator on request

Expensive

Audiotours, shop

HIGHLIGHTS

In the Salone Dorato:

- *Portrait of a Young Woman*, Piero del Pollaiolo—this lovely portrait has become a symbol of the palace
- *The Virgin and the Child*, Sandro Botticelli
- *St. Nicholas of Tolentino*, Piero della Francesca
- *Madonna and Child*, Andrea Mantegna
- Arms collection

The palace and its exquisite collection of paintings and decorative arts belonged to Gian Giacomo Poldi Pezzoli, a 19th-century Milanese aristocrat. Each room was planned to evoke a style of the past.

Stunning collection With the considerable fortune inherited from both sides of the family, Poldi Pezzoli (1822–79) amassed a large collection of antiques and art, including his remarkable armory. With the advice of leading experts, he built up a collection of armor, furniture, textiles, ceramics, bronzes and *objets d'art*. Pride of place, however, goes to his fabulous collection of paintings. On his death, he left the palace and its contents "to the use and benefit of the public". The building was badly bombed in 1943, but was rebuilt, retaining the original decoration where possible. Through gifts and bequests, the museum considerably enlarged its collection in the 1970s and 1980s.

Art and arms The two floors of exhibits are connected by a staircase with landscape paintings and a black marble fountain. The ground-floor rooms are devoted to the Armory, in its stunning neo-Gothic setting, the Fresco Room, the textile collections and library. The main collections are upstairs: paintings from the 14th- to 16th-century Lombard School, northern Italian works of art from the 14th to 18th centuries and the Salone Dorato, or Golden Room, with Renaissance masterpieces. There are also jewelry, sundials, clocks and watches.

Pinacoteca di Brera

The Brera gallery offers the chance to see one of the finest collections of northern Italian paintings. From small beginnings, it was enlarged by Napoleon to include works by the region's major artists.

Impressive collection The gallery is in Palazzo Brera, a baroque palace built on the site of a 14th-century Jesuit convent. Empress Maria Theresa of Austria evicted the Jesuits, redesigned the palace in neoclassical style and founded the Accademia di Belle Arti in 1773. The Pinacoteca opened in 1809, showing mostly works that had been confiscated by Napoleon from churches and convents in French-occupied territories: Lombardy, Veneto, Emilia-Romagna and the Marche. In 1882, the Accademia di Belle Arti and the Pinacoteca became independent, and the gallery became a state-owned art museum.

An art lover's heaven The works of art are arranged in 38 large rooms. Although the collection spans six centuries and includes some non-Italian artists (El Greco, Anthony Van Dyck, Rubens, Rembrandt), the emphasis is on northern Italian 15th- to 16th-century art. The collection is full of gems by the leading Renaissance masters, with the Venetian collection the largest and most important outside Venice. Here, too, you have a chance to study the Lombard masters of the Renaissance. The two most famous paintings in the collection are by Piero della Francesca and Raphael.

THE BASICS

brera.beniculturali.it

⊞ G4

✉ Via Brera 28, 20121

☎ 02 722 631

🕐 Tue, Wed, Fri–Sun 8.30–7.15, Thu 8.30am–10.15pm. Closed 1 Jan, 1 May, 25 Dec

🚇 Lanza, Montenapoleone

🚌 61; tram 1, 4, 12, 14, 27

♿ Good, elevator

💰 Moderate

ℹ Audiotours in English, book and souvenir shop

HIGHLIGHTS

● Jesi Collection—paintings and sculpture from the first half of the 19th century
● *Marriage of the Virgin* (1504), Raphael
● *Montefeltro Altarpiece* (1472–74), Piero della Francesca
● *Dead Christ*, Mantegna
● Portraits by Lotto, Tintoretto, Titian
● *Supper of Emmaus*, Caravaggio
● *The Kiss*, Francesco Hayez

Quadrilatero d'Oro

● Cova at Via Montenapoleone 8 (▷ 39), a historic café with tantalizing window displays of patisserie, sweets and chocolates. Sip coffee at the bar or sit in one of the smart salons with well-dressed Milanese
● One of the best spots in Europe to window shop
● Aristocratic residences

● Make an early start to avoid the crowds, but most shops won't open before 9.30am.

Milan is Italy's high spot for fashion and the area known as the Quadrilatero d'Oro (The Golden Quadrangle) is the most exclusive shopping quarter in the city. Whatever fashion designer you are looking for, you will find them here.

Glitz and glamor The Quadrilatero d'Oro is defined by Via Montenapoleone, Via Manzoni, Via della Spiga and Via Sant'Andrea. Via Manzoni is wide and traffic laden, the other streets in the shopping quarter are relatively quiet and make for pleasant shopping. Via Montenapoleone, familiarly known as Montenapo, is the most famous of these exclusive streets, flaunting world-famous designer names such as Ferragamo, Armani, Valentino, Prada and Versace, and high-class jewelers.

Palaces, courtyards and museums The name Quadrilatero d'Oro comes from the early 19th century and the quarter still preserves some of its historic *palazzi* as well as many fascinating courtyards. Via Bigli has the oldest buildings, with some of the palaces dating back to the 17th century. The shopping district is also home to the Museo Bagatti Valsecchi (▷ 27) and two civic museums, both at Via Sant'Andrea 6: the Museo di Milano (▷ 32–33) and the Museo di Storia Contemporanea (Contemporary History).

Milan style Don't expect a bargain unless you come during the January sales; the prices here tend to be higher than the rest of the city. The window fronts are stylish, artfully displaying the latest trends in fashion, as well as showcasing jewelry, fine leather, luxury furs and accessories.

THE BASICS

➕ H4

✉ 20121

🕐 Varied. Most shops close on Sun and Mon, though some are open on Mon afternoon. Most open at 9am or 9.30am

🍴 Numerous, with some very chic ones

🚇 San Babila, Montenapoleone

🚌 61, 94; tram 1, 2

♿ Good

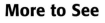

More to See

ARCHI DI PORTA NUOVA
This large, double-arched gateway separates Via Manzoni and Piazza Cavour. This and Porta Ticinese are the only surviving gates of the old medieval walls.

➕ H4 ✉ North end of Via Manzoni, 20121 Ⓜ Montenapoleone 🚌 61, 94; tram 1, 2

BASTIONI DI PORTA VENEZIA
On the site of one of the Porte Regie (Royal Gates) in the Spanish city walls, constructed in the 16th century, the present-day arch dates from 1828.

➕ K3 ✉ Piazza Oberdan, 20129 Ⓜ Porta Venezia 🚌 Tram 9, 29, 30

LIBERTY-STYLE ARCHITECTURE
Streets around Piazza Oberdan make up one of Milan's best areas for Liberty-style architecture, known outside Italy as art nouveau. Two good examples are on Via Malpighi, Nos. 3 and 12, and another is at Via Paolo Frisi 2, known as Palazzina Liberty. Heading south from Piazza Oberdan on Viale Piave, look for floral motifs at No. 42, one of Milan's best Liberty buildings, and also notice No. 11, the Casa Bossi, with its elaborate balconies.

➕ K4 ✉ Around Piazza Oberdan, 20129 Ⓜ Porta Venezia 🚌 Tram 9, 29, 30

MUSEO DEL RISORGIMENTO
museodelrisorgimento.mi.it
This museum is in the neoclassical Palazzo Moriggia and traces Italy's history from Napoleon's campaigns in Italy (1796 and 1800) to Unification in 1866. Exhibits include prints, paintings, documents, busts, mementoes and proclamations.

➕ H4 ✉ Via Borgonuovo 23, 20121 ☎ 02 8846 4173 ⏰ Tue–Sun 9–1, 2–5.30 Ⓜ Montenapoleone 🚌 41, 61; tram 1, 2 ♿ Good 💰 Moderate, free on Fri after 2

MUSEO DI MILANO
costumemodaimmagine.mi.it
Together with the Museo di Storia Contemporanea, an exhibition space for modern history and lectures, the Museo di Milano is located in the Palazzo Morando

Deer statues outside the Natural History Museum

Attendolo Bolognini. The rooms of the 18th-century palace display the original furniture and decor of a typical noble family's residence. On show are paintings, prints and objects from the 18th century until the end of the 19th century.

🞢 J5 ✉ Via Sant'Andrea 6, 20121 ☎ 02 8846 5735 🕙 Tue–Sun 9–1, 2–5.30 🚇 Montenapoleone 🚌 61, 94; tram 1, 2 ♿ Good 🎫 Free

MUSEO DI STORIA NATURALE

comune.milano.it/museostorianaturale
Occupying 23 rooms of a mock-Romanesque late-19th-century building on the edge of the Giardini Indro Montanelli, this museum has sections on geology, mineralogy, paleontology, zoology and habitats. Children will love the dinosaurs and life-size reproductions of crocodiles, snakes and sea creatures. Explanations in Italian only.

🞢 K4 ✉ Corso Venezia 55, 20121 ☎ 02 8846 3337 🕙 Tue–Sun 9–5.30 🚇 Palestro 🚌 Tram 9, 30 ♿ Good 🎫 Moderate, free on Tue after 2, daily after 4.30

PALAZZO SERBELLONI

fondazioneserbelloni.com
This neoclassical palace has played host to famous figures such as Napoleon and Josephine and Vittorio Emanuele II. Built in 1793, it was partially restored after bombings in World War II. During office hours, you can walk through the huge arched entrance to the frescoed loggia and arcaded courtyard.

🞢 J5 ✉ Corso Venezia 16, 20121 ☎ 02 7600 7687 🚇 San Babila 🚌 61

SAN MARCO

Built in 1254, the present church was founded on the site of the 12th-century church of San Marco. Designed in Romanesque style, it underwent major Gothic and baroque transformations and 19th-century restoration. The main portal, with bas-reliefs, and the tower, with decorative friezes, survive from the 13th-century church.

🞢 G4 ✉ Piazza San Marco 2, 20121 ☎ 02 2900 2598 🕙 Daily 7.30–1, 4–7.15 🚌 61, 43 ♿ Good (chapels have steps) 🎫 Free

Detail of the first vault in the presbytery of San Marco

From Retail to Calm

Window-shop in Milan's bustling fashion quarter and then take a well-earned rest in the public gardens.

DISTANCE: 3.2km (2 miles) **ALLOW:** Half a day to include shopping and sights

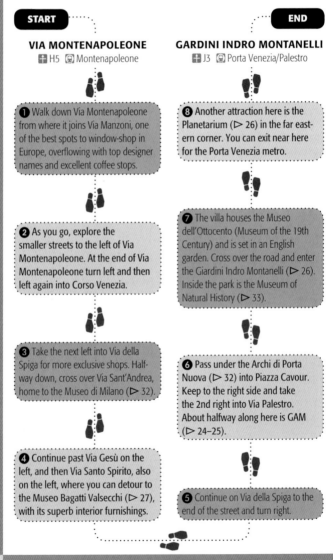

START

VIA MONTENAPOLEONE
🟩 H5 🚇 Montenapoleone

1 Walk down Via Montenapoleone from where it joins Via Manzoni, one of the best spots to window-shop in Europe, overflowing with top designer names and excellent coffee stops.

2 As you go, explore the smaller streets to the left of Via Montenapoleone. At the end of Via Montenapoleone turn left and then left again into Corso Venezia.

3 Take the next left into Via della Spiga for more exclusive shops. Half-way down, cross over Via Sant'Andrea, home to the Museo di Milano (▷ 32).

4 Continue past Via Gesù on the left, and then Via Santo Spirito, also on the left, where you can detour to the Museo Bagatti Valsecchi (▷ 27), with its superb interior furnishings.

END

GARDINI INDRO MONTANELLI
🟩 J3 🚇 Porta Venezia/Palestro

8 Another attraction here is the Planetarium (▷ 26) in the far eastern corner. You can exit near here for the Porta Venezia metro.

7 The villa houses the Museo dell'Ottocento (Museum of the 19th Century) and is set in an English garden. Cross over the road and enter the Giardini Indro Montanelli (▷ 26). Inside the park is the Museum of Natural History (▷ 33).

6 Pass under the Archi di Porta Nuova (▷ 32) into Piazza Cavour. Keep to the right side and take the 2nd right into Via Palestro. About halfway along here is GAM (▷ 24–25).

5 Continue on Via della Spiga to the end of the street and turn right.

THE NORTHEAST WALK

Shopping

ACQUA DI PARMA

acquadiparma.com

One of Italy's most iconic labels produces high-end and classic fragrances, body and facial products, beautifully packaged in the house style.

J5 ✉ 1 Via Gesù, 20121 ☎ 02 7602 3307 Ⓜ Montenapoleone

ALAN JOURNO

alanjourno.com

Crazy bags, hats and lots more in eccentric styles displayed around a stainless steel and glass staircase that spirals over three levels.

J4 ✉ Via della Spiga 36, 20121 ☎ 02 7600 1309 Ⓜ Montenapoleone

ALESSI

alessi.com

Alessi has been commissioning the world's leading designers for nearly 100 years, resulting in some of the best home and kitchenware available.

H4 ✉ Via Manzoni 14–16, 20121 ☎ 02 795 726 Ⓜ Montenapoleone

ANTICHITÀ CAIATI

caiati.it

This prestigious gallery deals in Old Master paintings and sculpture. It also sells contemporary art, ephemera and furniture, and publishes monographs and catalogs.

J5 ✉ Via Gesú 17, 20121 ☎ 02 794 866 Ⓜ Montenapoleone

ARTEMIDE

artemide.com

Renowned for forthright modern designs for the home, created by top designers, the products are displayed to best effect in a gallery-like showroom.

J5 ✉ Corso Monforte 19, 20122 ☎ 02 7600 6930 Ⓜ San Babila

ASPESI

aspesi.com

Italians love this label for its laid-back, sporty elegance and practicality. Shop here for understated, practical sport and weekend wear.

J4 ✉ Via Verri 5, 20121 ☎ 02 7602 2478 Ⓜ Montenapoleone

BOTTEGA VENETA

bottegaveneta.com

The well-known name in Italian fashion opened this immense "maison" branch in 2013 as a second sales point to its flagship store on Via Montenapoleone. It carries the entire range, in an 18th-century *palazzo*.

J5 ✉ Via Sant'Andrea 15, 20121 ☎ 02 7787 8115 Ⓜ San Babila

BVLGARI

bulgari.com

It's the unmistakable style that's the hallmark of Bvlgari. Here you'll find the full range—accessories, eyewear, fragrances and designer watches and jewelry.

J4 ✉ Via della Spiga angolo Via Sant'Andrea, 20121 ☎ 02 777 001 Ⓜ Montenapoleone

EMPIRE OF ARMANI

Milan-born designer Giorgio Armani began his career as a window dresser at the city's La Rinascente department store, and in 1961 progressed to the menswear shop Nino Cerruti. In 1975, Armani branched out alone, and within 10 years had become a household name when he revolutionized the industry with his more wearable and less-expensive collection. There is a contemporary fashion art museum, Armani Silos, dedicated to the label (✉ Via Bergognone 4, 20144 ☎ 02 9163 0010; armani.com/silos/en Ⓦ Wed–Sun 11–7).

DAMIANI

damiani.com

Damiani have been creating bold designs using high-quality gems since 1924. Also classy watches, strings of pearls and fine wedding rings.

➕ J5 ✉ Via Montenapoleone 10, 20121 ☎ 02 7602 8088 🚇 San Babila

DE PADOVA

depadova.com

The full range of home furnishings reflects the company's commitment to modern design with a retro twist.

➕ J5 ✉ Corso Venezia 14, 20121 ☎ 02 777 201 🚇 San Babila, Palestro

DMAGAZINE OUTLET

dmag.eu

One of the most central of Milan's high-fashion discount stores, selling end-of-season shop, boutique and warehouse returns and some seconds from top designers, with reductions of anything from 50–70 percent.

➕ H4 ✉ Via Manzoni 44, 20121 ☎ 02 3651 4365 🚇 Montenapoleone

DOLCE & GABBANA

dolcegabbana.it

At the cutting edge of fashion and straight off the catwalk, this store is worth a look for the decor alone.

➕ J4 ✉ Via della Spiga 26 20121 ☎ 02 7600 1155 🚇 Montenapoleone

DROGHERIA PARINI

parini1915.com

Upstairs for mouthwatering confection-ery and downstairs to the arched cellar for wines and spirits, organic jams and jellies, compotes and chutneys, and excellent blends of coffee and tea—all beautifully gift-wrapped. Very friendly and helpful staff.

➕ H4 ✉ Via Borgospesso 1, 20121 ☎ 02 3668 3500 🚇 Montenapoleone

FELTRINELLI

lafeltrinelli.it

This big branch of Italy's most famous bookstore chain is stocked with the best and most up-to-date publications. There's an excellent range of foreign books, guides, maps and foreign-language magazines.

➕ H4 ✉ Via Manzoni 12, 20121 ☎ 02 7600 0618 🚇 Montenapoleone

FENDI

fendi.com

Edoardo Fendi and his wife Adele founded a small leatherware shop in Rome in 1925; their five daughters went on to develop it into a powerful fashion empire, and this flagship store focuses on women's wear, bags, shoes and accessories.

➕ J5 ✉ Via Montenapoleone 3, 20121 ☎ 02 7602 1617 🚇 San Babila

FLOS

flos.com

High-quality ultramodern lighting for the home and office, with contemporary

---

WOMEN'S HATS

Although women from an early stage were expected to cover their heads, it was not until the 17th century that women's head-gear began to emerge as a fashion item. The word "milliner"—a maker of women's hats—was first recorded in 1529, when it referred to the products for which Milan was Europe's leading manufacturer—ribbons and gloves. The Milanese haber-dashers who imported such fineries were called "Millaners", from which the word was derived.

creations by names such as Philippe Starck and Jasper Morrison.

🔲 J5 ✉ Corso Monforte 9, 20122 ☎ 02 3701 1080 🚇 San Babila

FRATELLI ROSSETTI

rossetti.it

This family company, founded 30 years ago by the brothers Renzo and Renato, pushes Salvatore Ferragamo (▷ right) for the title of Italy's best shoe store, with slightly lower prices than its rival.

🔲 J5 ✉ Via Montenapoleone 1, 20121 ☎ 02 7602 1650 🚇 San Babila

MIU MIU

miumiu.com

Child of Prada, Miu Miu's trademark is urban chic and nods to retro style both in cut and fabrics. Collections include street, daytime and casual wear, all showcased in the brilliantly designed hi-tech store, where shoes, bags, eyewear and fragrances are also on offer.

🔲 J5 ✉ Via Sant'Andrea 21, 20121 ☎ 02 7600 1799 🚇 San Babila

LA PERLA

laperla.it

Beautiful lingerie and sleepwear, featuring gossamer silk, the smoothest satin and lace and silk ribbon trim, are the hallmarks of this quintessential Italian label. This store stocks a fine range, including swimwear and collections with a single decorative theme.

🔲 J5 ✉ Via Montenapoleone 14, 20121 ☎ 02 7600 0460 🚇 San Babila

PELLINI

pellini.it

The Pellini family have been making idiosyncratic, one-off costume jewelry for three generations, and this store is Donatella Pellini's baby. You'll find hats, scarves and bags, as well as the trademark resin and glass jewelry—quirky, covetable and surprisingly affordable.

🔲 H4 ✉ Via Manzoni 20, 20121 ☎ 02 7600 8084 🚇 Montenapoleone

SALVATORE FERRAGAMO

ferragamo.com

Italy's most famous shoe designer, whose stores grace exclusive shopping streets all over the world.

🔲 J5 ✉ Via Montenapoleone 3, 20121 ☎ 02 7600 0054 🚇 San Babila

SERMONETA

sermonetagloves.com

Gloves made in leather, wool and silk, lined with cashmere or rabbit fur, in every color, with every possible decoration are available here. Style and colors change in tune with the seasons.

🔲 J5 ✉ Via della Spiga 46, 20121 ☎ 02 7631 8303 🚇 San Babila

VETRERIE DI EMPOLI

vetreriediempoli.it

Jewel-rich colors, exquisite engraving and gold-leaf decoration feature in this stunning and very high-end store. They sell glasses, decanters, dishes, fruit and cake stands, jugs and chandeliers.

🔲 J4 ✉ Via Montenapoleone 22, 20121 ☎ 02 7600 8791 🚇 Montenapoleone

DESIGNER HEAVEN

The concentration of designer stores in the Quadrilatero d'Oro is unbelievable. Check out Via Manzoni for Armani; Via Sant'Andrea for Chanel and Prada; Via Montenapoleone for Gucci, Louis Vuitton, Versace and Trussardi, and don't forget one of Italy's preferred sons, Roberto Cavalli, with his signature animal-skin designs on Via della Spiga.

Entertainment and Nightlife

ANTEO

spaziocinema.info

One of Milan's leading original-language cinemas, with an emphasis on art house. Films from countries such as Sweden, Japan or France are often shown with English subtitles.

🔖 G4 ✉ Via Milazzo 9, 20121 ☎ 02 659 7732 🚇 Moscova

THE FRIENDS

thefriendspubmilano.it

This is where to go if you are feeling nostalgic for a British pub; the building was even sent in parts from England. Lots of Victoriana decor and all the beers and lagers you could want.

🔖 J3 ✉ Viale Monte Santo 12, 20124 ☎ 02 2900 5315 🚇 Repubblica

HCLUB DIANA GARDEN

Partake of sophisticated cocktails and aperitifs in the bar at the Sheraton Diana Majestic hotel (▷ 112). Sit out in the elegant gardens during summer, while the lavish lounge and opulent bar are a great pit-stop in the cooler months.

🔖 K4 ✉ Viale Piave 42, 20129 ☎ 02 2058 2081 🚇 Porta Venezia

LELEPHANTE

One of the city's leading hangouts for dressed-up partyers and trendy students. Decked out with innovative plastic furniture. Aimed at both the straight and gay crowd.

🔖 L4 ✉ Via Melzo 22, 20129 ☎ 02 2951 8768 🚇 Porta Venezia

PISCINA COZZI

Located on the tree-lined Viale Tunisia just north of the Giardini Indro Montanelli, this swimming pool complex has two pools, one of which is Olympic size with 5m (16ft) and 10m (33ft) diving boards. It can get crowded in high season but it is the closest place in central Milan to cool off. Open every day but check in advance for session times.

🔖 K3 ✉ Via Tunisia 35, 20124 ☎ 02 659 9703 🚇 Porta Venezia, Repubblica

SALA VENEZIA

This huge retro dance hall has a timeless charm, where Milanese of all ages come to boogie the night away.

🔖 K3 ✉ Via Alvise Cadamosto 2, 20129 ☎ 02 204 3765 🚇 Porta Venezia

TEATRO MANZONI

teatromanzoni.it

This theater is particularly popular with the Milanese and produces a variety of performances, including serious drama such as plays by Chekhov and Brecht, Italian plays, one-person shows, stand-up comedy, classical music concerts and musicals; come on Sunday morning for jazz.

🔖 H4 ✉ Via Manzoni 42, 20121 ☎ 02 0063 4555 🚇 Montenapoleone

TICKET INFORMATION

Tickets for plays and concerts can be booked through agencies or more easily online via Milano Tickets (milanooperatickets.com or ☎ 4319 688 622), Ticket One (ticketone.it or ☎ 892101) or Viva Ticket (vivaticket.it or ☎ 892 2324); all will charge a commission. The concert, theater and opera seasons run roughly from Sep/Oct to May/Jun. Tickets for La Scala must be booked well in advance (teatroallascala.ticketone.it). It may be possible to buy a ticket for the same day: they go on sale simultaneously online and at the ticket office in Largo Ghiringhelli (on the left of the theater facade) at 9am daily.

Where to Eat

PRICES

Prices are approximate, based on a
3-course meal for one person.

€€€   over €55
€€   €25–€55
€   under €25

LE 5 TERRE (€€–€€€)

ristorantele5terre.com

In business for more than 20 years,
this restaurant is the master of Ligurian
cuisine, particularly renowned for its fish
and seafood dishes, athough carnivores
are catered for. The surroundings are
elegant and the excellent wine list
comprehensive. Leave room for the
delicious desserts.

➕ H3 ✉ Via Andrea Appiani 9, 20121
☎ 02 657 5177 ⏲ Sun–Fri lunch; daily dinner
🚇 Repubblica, Turati

BICE (€€)

bicemilano.it

Founded in 1926, Bice is on one of the
smartest streets in the fashion district.
Extensive à la carte menu; lighter set
menu for lunch.

➕ H4 ✉ Via Borgospesso 12, 20121
☎ 02 7600 2572 ⏲ Mon–Sat lunch, dinner
🚇 Montenapoleone

BORGOSPESSO 1 (€€)

borgospesso1.com

The successor to the famous Bagutta,
Borgospesso's intimately lit dining space
is sited in the crypt of a disused church,
also home to a sleek bar-cum-bistro and
a tempting delicatessen. The food
retains its punch, with carefully sourced
ingredients used to create Milanese
classics, some with a modern twist.

➕ H4 ✉ Via Borgospesso 1, 20121 ☎ 02
3668 3500 ⏲ Mon–Sat lunch, dinner
🚇 Montenapoleone

CORSIA DEL GIARDINO (€–€€)

corsiadelgiardino.it

Old concept, new style: this is a light,
sleek, all-day eatery overlooking a green
courtyard, where the choice kicks off
with a light breakfast or hearty brunch
and continues throughout the day.
Imaginative courses—try the sushi or
beef carpaccio–give way to light snacks,
teatime treats and savories.

➕ H4 ✉ Via Manzoni 16, 20121 ☎ 02 7628
0726 ⏲ Daily all day 🚇 Montenapoleone

COVA (€€)

pasticceriacova.com

In business since 1817, this landmark
café is an ideal stop for a break from
shopping. It is expensive but the coffee
and cakes are irresistible.

➕ H5 ✉ Via Montenapoleone 8, 20121
☎ 02 7600 5599 ⏲ Mon–Sat all day 🚇 San
Babila, Montenapoleone

DAL BOLOGNESE (€€€)

dalbolognese.it

Packed with a glitzy Milanese crowd—
fashion and media folk and football
players. The food is strictly Bolognese:
homemade pastas, meats and great
desserts. Eat outside in the fine weather.

➕ J3 ✉ Via Amedei 8, 20123 ☎ 02
6269 4845 ⏲ Closed Sat lunch and Sun
🚇 Repubblica

ANYONE FOR COFFEE?

The Milanese have coffees to suit different
types of food or to be drunk at different
times of day. Cappuccinos are often the
choice at breakfast and never drunk by
Italians after lunch or dinner. This is followed by espresso for a shot of caffeine
later in the day. Not many visitors will
risk the *ristretto*, as this is the strongest
of them all.

JOIA (€€€)

joia.it

Closeness to nature is the philosophy behind this first-class vegetarian restaurant, where the freshest of ingredients are lovingly prepared to tempt the palate.

🔢 K3 ✉ Via P. Castaldi 18, 20124 ☎ 02 2952 2124 🕐 Mon–Sat lunch, dinner. Closed 3 weeks Aug 🚇 Repubblica, Porta Venezia

LA LATTERIA (€–€€)

Busy family-run restaurant serving food from the Lombardy region. Haunt of journalists and the occasional celebrity in search of home cooking.

🔢 G3 ✉ Via San Marco 24, 20121 ☎ 02 659 7653 🕐 Mon–Fri lunch, dinner 🚇 Moscova

NOBU (€€€)

noburestaurants.com

Chef Nobuyuki Matsuhisa has been creating culinary treats for more than 10 years in the Armani store. Japanese cuisine meets South American and Californian influences. Very smart and very expensive.

🔢 H4 ✉ Via G. Pisoni 1, 20121 ☎ 02 6231 2645 🕐 Mon–Sat lunch, dinner; Sun dinner only 🚇 Montenapoleone

RANGOLI (€)

rangoli.it.

Authentic North Indian cuisine in the Brera district. The dishes cooked in the *tandoor* (clay oven) are particularly popular. There is a good vegetarian menu.

🔢 G3 ✉ Via Solferino 36, 20121 ☎ 02 2900 5333 🕐 Tue–Fri lunch, dinner; Sat–Mon dinner only 🚇 Moscova

SANTINI (€€€)

This is the epitome of sophistication with cool, clean lines and modern lighting. The striking blue-and-white dining room is very distinctive. A full menu features fusion and Piedmont cuisine, or try light lunch options such as spaghetti or vegetable wraps. Alternatively you can opt for the special "Taste of Santini" menu featuring the chef's specials. There's a covered garden for alfresco eating.

🔢 G3 ✉ Via San Marco 3, 20121 ☎ 02 655 5587 🕐 Mon–Fri lunch, dinner; Sat lunch only 🚇 Lanza

SOLFERINO (€€)

ilsolferino.com

One of the oldest restaurants in the city, which serves excellent Milanese dishes in beautiful surroundings. Meat and fish dishes are to the fore, but there are also good choices for vegetarians.

🔢 H3 ✉ Via Castelfidardo 2, 20121 ☎ 02 2900 5748 🕐 Daily lunch, dinner 🚇 Moscova

LA TAVERNETTA DA ELIO (€€)

tavernetta.it

In the same family since 1957, this restaurant is preferred by celebrities and literary types. The cuisine is Tuscan in its most traditional forms—thick soups, pastas and hearty meat dishes. Tuscan wines and good desserts.

🔢 H4 ✉ Via Fatebenefratelli 30, 20121 ☎ 02 653 441 🕐 Mon–Fri lunch, dinner; Sat dinner only 🚇 Montenapoleone, San Babila

---

ITALIAN ICE CREAM

The Italians justifiably pride themselves on their superior ice cream, and Milan regards itself as one of the best ice-cream-making areas in the country. There are *gelaterie* dating back to the mid-19th century that are still in business; some have as many as 100 different varieties on offer.

Centro Storico

Here is the heart of historic Milan and the meeting place for tourists and locals alike. The Piazza del Duomo is dominated by the splendid wedding-cake of a cathedral, the third largest in the world.

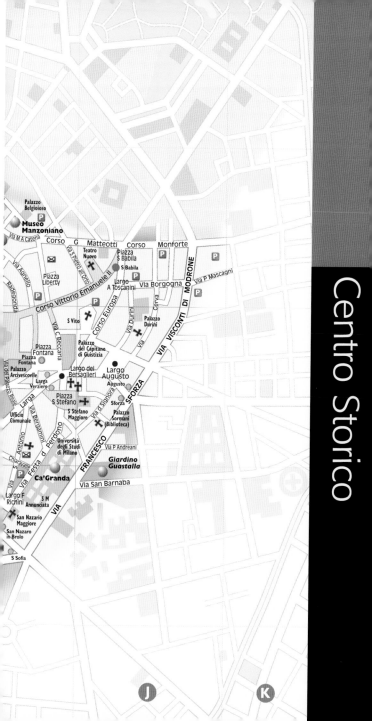

Palazzo Belgioioso

Museo Manzoniano

Via M A Catena

Corso G Matteotti   Corso   Monforte

Via S Paolo all'Orto

Teatro Nuovo

Piazza S Babila

S Babila

Piazza Liberty

Corso Vittorio Emanuele II

Largo A Toscanini   Via Borgogna

Via Durini

Via P Mascagni

VIA VISCONTI DI MODRONE

S Vito

Corso Europa

Via Durini

Cerva

Palazzo Durini

Via

Via C Beccaria

Palazzo del Capitano di Giustizia

Piazza Fontana

Piazza Fontana

Largo dei Bersaglieri

Largo Augusto

Palazzo Arcivescovile

Larga Verziere

Piazza S Stefano

S Stefano Maggiore

Augusto

SFORZA

Sforza

Via d Signora

Ufficio Comunale

Via Bergamini

Via Larga

Palazzo Sormani (Biblioteca)

Via d Palazzo Reale

Via Antonio

Chiaravalle

Via Festa d Perdono

Università degli Studi di Milano

FRANCESCO

Via P Andreani

Giardino Guastalla

Largo F Richini

Ca'Granda

S M Annunciata

VIA

Via San Barnaba

San Nazario Maggiore

San Nazaro in Brolo

S Sofia

J   K

Duomo

HIGHLIGHTS

- The roof and the view
- The apse
- Stained-glass windows
- Trivulzio Candelabra (12th-century, crafted in gold)
- Treasury's collection of gold and silverwork
- The elaborate crypt

TIP

- Take the guided tour, which includes a tour of the cathedral, the archeological area, baptistery and roof-tops and terraces.

Symbol of the city, the sumptuous Duomo, with its huge proportions, towers over the Piazza del Duomo. An ascent to the roof reveals a wonderful panorama of Milan and beyond.

Dazzling and ethereal The Duomo bristles with Gothic statues, gargoyles, pinnacles and soaring spires and has attracted comments from the censorious "an imitation hedgehog" (D.H. Lawrence) to the lyrical "a poem of marble" (Mark Twain). Ascend to the roof, by steps or elevator, for a wonderful panorama of Milan and, on a clear day, a view as far as the Alps.

Controversial building Milan's Duomo was founded in 1386 under the ambitious Gian Galeazzo Visconti, who resolved to build the

Clockwise from far left: the elaborate towers of Milan's extraordinary cathedral; the structure dominates Piazza del Duomo; soaring columns inside the Duomo; detail of the intricate stonework

biggest church in Italy. Although the church was consecrated in 1418, it remained incomplete for more than four centuries. Work finally started on the facade in the early 17th century, but was only finished in 1812, under Napoleon.

Into the darkness The Duomo is 157m (515ft) long, 33m (108ft) wide across the nave and 92m (302ft) wide across the transept; the roof is decorated with 2,245 statues, 135 spires and 96 gargoyles; the interior can hold 40,000 people. It is topped by a copper statue, the Madonnina, (Little Madonna). After the stunning white exterior, the interior feels gloomy, but your eye is drawn to the stained-glass windows. Monuments include the statue of *The Flayed San Bartolomeo* (1562), with his skin draped over his shoulders.

THE BASICS

duomomilano.it

✚ H6

✉ Piazza del Duomo, 20121

☎ 02 7202 3375

🕐 Cathedral daily 7–6.30. Baptistery San Giovanni alle Fonti 10–6; closed 1 Jan, 1 May, 15 Aug, 25 Dec. Terraces 9–6. Baptistery of San Stefano daily 9–7; closed 1 May, 25 Dec (enter North lift)

🚇 Duomo

🚃 Tram 1, 2, 3, 15, 24 and others

♿ Main cathedral good. Crypt and Treasury none

🎫 Cathedral free (fee for photography). S .Giovanni moderate; terraces expensive; S. Stefano free

Fondazione Prada

HIGHLIGHTS

● The Torre
● Work by Jeff Koons and Damien Hirst in the *Atlas* exhibition rooms
● Wes Anderson's Bar Luce
● The views from different floors

TIPS

● Leave time for refreshment in the Bar Luce.
● Take time to examine the exterior before entering.
● Check out what's on at the cinema.

A once-dilapidated factory has been revamped and extended as a nine-story contemporary art space, hosting both the Fondazione Prada's permanent collection and changing exhibitions by leading Italian and international artists.

The project In 2015 the first stage of the transformation of a cluster of old distillery buildings into a multilevel exhibition space was completed by the Fondazione Prada, the art foundation attached to the eponymous fashion label. The Fondazione now displays contemporary art, stages exhibitions and hosts film screenings, performances and events. Miuccia Prada, granddaughter of the founder of the fashion label, then commissioned architect Rem Koolhaas of OMA to design the Torre, the

Left to right: architect Rem Koolhaas's Torre towers above the Fondazione Prada; one of the foundation's stunning exhibition rooms

central architectural feature, a new addition to the Milanese skyline, which opened in 2018.

Architecture for the 21st century For many it's the architecture that steals the show, with a compound of warehouses, distillery sheds and laboratories dating from 1910 transformed into an edgy post-industrial space drenched with light. At the heart of this is the Torre, a brand new building in the shape of a white concrete tower, whose nine floors alternate in shape between rectangular and trapezoid

The works The permanent collection, under the umbrella title of *Atlas*, has works and installations by artists such as Anish Kapoor, Damien Hirst, Mario Sironi and Nathalie Djurberg, as well as temporary shows.

THE BASICS

fondazioneprada.org
🚌 Off map at H8
✉ Largo Isarco 2, 20139
☎ 02 5666 2611
🕐 Daily 10–9
🍴 Restaurant and bar
Ⓜ Piazza Lodi
🚌 77, 90, 91; tram 24
♿ Good
💰 Expensive (includes Osservatorio in Galleria Vittorio Emanuele II)

Galleria Vittorio Emanuele II

HIGHLIGHTS

- Watching the fashionable Milanese
- Savini restaurant (▷ 60)
- Camparino in Galleria—have a cocktail or a coffee in the famous period café (▷ 59)
- Excellent boutique shopping

Linking Piazza del Duomo and Piazza della Scala, this elegant glass-roofed arcade has long been a popular meeting point for the Milanese. It's worth having a pricey cappuccino just to watch the perpetual parade of stylish locals.

City reconstruction It was in 1865, after Unification, that the architect Giuseppe Mengoni offered his silver trowel to King Vittorio Emanuele II —after whom the arcade was named—to lay the foundation stone of the Galleria. Sadly, Mengoni fell to his death from the scaffolding a few days before the inauguration in 1897. The project's completion, in 1898, was marked by the building of a triumphal arch at the Duomo end. The creation of the arcade, an affirmation of the existence

The Galleria is perfect for a stroll, to window-shop or pause for a sophisticated break and to admire the stunning glass roof

of a unified Italy, and the colossal demolition process that it involved reshaped the whole structure of the city.

Glitzy Milan This is a great place for shopping, eating and drinking—if you can afford it. The glass roof gives the arcade a feeling of light and space, even on a dull day. There are excellent bookshops, music stores and leather and clothes boutiques. A focal point is the central octagon area, under the glass dome, 47m (154ft) high, with ornate pavement mosaics, depicting city symbols, below. Above this octagon you'll find the Osservatorio Prada, an outpost of the Fondazione Prada (▷ 46–47), dedicated to temporary photographic shows. At ground level once more is Savini (▷ 60), a famous restaurant.

THE BASICS

✚ H5

✉ Galleria Vittorio Emanuele II, 20121

☎ 02 7740 4343

🕐 Most shops daily 9am– 10pm; some close 2–4

🍽 Plenty (▷ opposite)

🚇 Duomo

🚌 61; tram 1, 2, 3, 14, 15, 24

♿ Good

Osservatorio Prada
fondazioneprada.org

🕐 Mon, Wed–Fri 2–8, Sat–Sun 11–8

💲 Expensive

Palazzo Reale

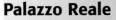

TOP 25

Today's Palazzo Reale is a cultural center and home to exhibitions

THE BASICS

palazzorealemilan.it

⊞ H6

✉ Piazza del Duomo 12, 20122

☎ 02 860 165

🕐 Palazzo Reale: Mon 2.30–7.30, Tue–Wed, Fri 9.30–7.30, Thu, Sat, 9.30am–10.30pm. Museo del Duomo Tue–Sun 10–6. Closed 1 Jan, 1 May, 15 Aug, 25 Dec

🚇 Duomo

🚌 54; tram 1, 2, 3, 12, 14, 15, 16, 19, 23, 24, 27

♿ Good

💶 Palazzo Reale expensive. Museo del Duomo moderate

ℹ Palazzo Reale bookshop for temporary exhibitions only

HIGHLIGHTS

- Museo della Reggia
- Restored apartments
- Films and concerts in the palace courtyards in summer

In the heart of the city, overshadowed by the Duomo, this site has held the 11th-century council building, the ducal residence of the Viscontis and Sforzas, and royal palace of the Austrian rulers.

A plethora of museums The palazzo has been rebuilt several times, the present-day building owing its neoclassical appearance to the 1770s redevelopment of the square. Inside you can see the superbly restored state rooms, one of which, the Sala delle Cariatidi, remains as it was at the end of World War II. Your visit may coincide with a blockbuster art show.

History of art The 11th-century Palazzo Broletto Vecchio (Courthouse) was rebuilt by the ruling Viscontis between 1330 and 1336, and redesigned in the 16th century by the Sforzas. Mozart performed at the hall here in 1770, when he was 14. In the following decade the palace was rebuilt by Giuseppe Piermarini. Large sections of the palace were demolished in the 1920s and 1930s, and most of its dazzling interior was destroyed in the bombings of 1943. In the 1960s, the city bought the palace for use as museums, offices and to display art exhibitions. CIMAC was housed here in 1983, but has now closed and its fine collection of paintings with works by Picasso and Matisse has moved to GAM (▷ 24–25). The Museo del Duomo, next to the Palazzo Reale, charts the history of the cathedral and was reopened in 2013.

The inner courtyard of the Pinacoteca Ambrosiana

Pinacoteca Ambrosiana

Cardinal Federico Borromeo built the Palazzo Ambrosiana in 1608 to house his collection of books. The art collection includes outstanding works by 15th- and 16th-century Italian and Flemish masters.

Phenomenal collection In the 17th century, Cardinal Federico Borromeo commissioned eight experts to travel through Europe and the Middle East to amass a collection for his library. The Biblioteca Ambrosiana was set up with around 30,000 prints and 14,000 manuscripts. Nine years later, his personal collection of 127 paintings was added to form the Pinacoteca Ambrosiana. The building was extended in the 19th century. From 1990 to 1997 the gallery closed for radical restructure; 10 new rooms were made accessible, enabling around 400 paintings to be displayed. Works by Leonardo, Titian, Raphael and Caravaggio are among those exhibited.

Essential viewing The ground-floor library has more than 1,000 pages of drawings by Leonardo da Vinci—only accessible to scholars. On the first floor, rooms 1 and 4–7 display the Borromeo collection: Tuscan, Lombard and Venetian Renaissance and 17th-century Flemish art. The drawings displayed under glass are Leonardo reproductions. Rooms 2 and 3 display Renaissance masterpieces. Rooms 8–24 have 14th- to 20th-century paintings, sculpture and *objets d'art*, culminating in Manfredo Settala's diverse scientific collection.

THE BASICS

ambrosiana.eu

⊞ G6

✉ Piazza Pio X1, 20123

☎ 02 806 921

🕑 Tue–Sun 10–6. Closed 1 Jan, Easter, Christmas

🚇 Cordusio, Duomo

🚊 Tram 2, 3, 14, 16, 24

♿ Good

💶 Expensive

ℹ Guidebooks and catalogs; shop sells good art books

HIGHLIGHTS

● Room 1: *Adoration of the Magi*, Titian
● Room 2: *The Musician*, school of Leonardo da Vinci
● Room 5: Raphael's cartoon for the *School of Athens* (1510), representing the greatest philosophers and mathematicians in conference
● Room 6: Caravaggio's staggeringly realistic *Basket of Fruit* (1594)

Santa Maria presso San Satiro

Inside Santa Maria presso San Satiro (left); view of the church's facade (right)

THE BASICS

✚ G6
✉ Via Torino 19, 20123
☎ 02 874 683
🕐 Tue–Sat 9.30–5.30, Sun 2.30–5.30
Ⓜ Duomo
🚋 Tram 2, 3, 14, 15, 16, 24
♿ Good
🎟 Free

HIGHLIGHTS

● The *trompe l'oeil* apse
● The 10th-century campanile, one of the oldest in Milan
● The dagger, used to desecrate the fresco of the Madonna

TIP

● Be sure to stand to one side of the main altar to appreciate the *trompe l'oeil* effect.

This 15th-century church is the work of Milan's most renowned Renaissance architect, Donato Bramante. Come here to experience an astounding optical illusion, where painted perspective is used to create depth where none exists.

An ancient foundation San Satiro was the brother of St. Ambrose, the patron saint of Milan, and was particularly revered by Bishop Anspert, who died in 876. He left funds for the construction of a church dedicated to the saint; all that remains of this is the Greek Cross Cappella della Pietà.

The miracle By the 13th century the church was famous for an image of the Virgin Mary, which was said to have bled when attacked with a knife by a maniac in 1242. Pilgrims flocked to see the image, which is still visible on the high altar, and it was decided that a new and fitting church should be built.

The Renaissance church In 1472 Duke Galeazzo Sforza commissioned Donato Bramante to draw up the plans. Bramante was constrained by space and came up with the idea to use painted perspective behind the main altar to give the illusion of space and depth. Stand at the entrance of the church and your eye is led down the barrel-vaulted central nave to the high altar and what appears to be a deep apse behind it. This *trompe l'oeil* is in fact only 97cm (38in) deep.

Teatro alla Scala

La Scala, commissioned by Empress Maria Theresa of Austria, has seen the premieres of many great classical Italian operas. The facade on Piazza della Scala is surprisingly sober, and belies the sumptuous auditorium.

World famous The opera house was built in 1776–78 by Giuseppe Piermarini, architect of the Palazzo Reale, and took the place of the smaller Teatro Regio Ducale, which had been destroyed by fire. After the 1943 bombings, La Scala was the first of the city's monuments to be rebuilt. It reopened in 1946 and was re-inaugurated by Toscanini, who came back from America after 17 years, having fled from Fascist Italy in 1929. Musical works by Rossini, Donizetti, Bellini, Verdi and Puccini had their debuts here, not always to great acclaim—the first night of Puccini's *Madama Butterfly* in 1904 was a complete fiasco—no one liked it!

Sumptuous interior The plush auditorium is decorated in red velvet and gilded stuccowork, with a 365-lamp crystal chandelier; it has an overall seating capacity of 2,015. You can view the auditorium as part of a museum tour. The Museo Teatrale alla Scala (▷ 54) contains a huge collection of theatrical memorabilia.

Major overhaul The opera house was revamped between 2002 and 2004, when the stage was completely rebuilt and the sound quality enhanced.

THE BASICS

teatroallascala.org
✚ H5
✉ Piazza della Scala, 20121
☎ La Scala Information Point and La Scala Bookstore (Piazza della Scala 5) 02 7200 3744
🕐 Opera season opening night always 7 Dec, feast day of Sant'Ambrogio, patron saint of Milan
Ⓜ Duomo, Cordusio
🚌 61; tram 1, 2
💵 Varies for performances; museum moderate
♿ Good

DID YOU KNOW?

● The opera house has exceptionally fine acoustics.
● The stage is one of the largest in the world, measuring 1,200sq m (13,000sq ft).
● Most of the world's best-known conductors and opera singers have performed here.
● Tickets are notoriously hard to get, so book well in advance (▷ 38, panel).

CENTRO STORICO TOP 25

More to See

CA' GRANDA

The vast Renaissance–Gothic building known as Ca' Granda was once a hospital. Founded by Francesco Sforza in the 15th century, construction continued from 1429 to 1797, with elegant courtyards and new blocks added. It became part of the University of Milan following restoration after World War II bombing.

➕ H7 ✉ Via Festa del Perdono 20121 ☎ 02 503 111 🕐 Mon–Fri 8–6, Sat 8–12.30 🚇 Missori 🚌 54, 77, 94; tram 12, 16, 23 🎟 Free

CORSO PORTA ROMANA

The ancient route to Rome started at the Porta Romana (Roman Gate). One of the city's busiest streets, it is lined with small shops, patisseries and cafés. The buildings of architectural interest, neoclassical and flamboyant art nouveau *palazzi*, lie toward the Piazza Missori end.

➕ H7 ✉ 20121 🚇 Missori, Crocetta, Porta Romana 🚌 77; tram 24

Statue on the Palazzo della Ragione

GIARDINO GUASTALLA

The oldest public gardens in Milan, founded in 1555 by Paola Ludovica Torelli, Countess of Guastalla, who planned it as part of the Guastalla College for daughters of impoverished local nobles, has several monuments and a fish pond.

➕ J7 ✉ Via San Barnaba, 20122 🕐 Daily 7–7 (longer hours in summer) 🚌 60, 77; tram 12, 27

MUSEO MANZONIANO

casadelmanzoni.it

Overlooking Piazza Belgioioso in the heart of the city, this was the home of Alessandro Manzoni, considered the greatest Italian novelist of the 19th century. Born in Milan, he lived here almost continuously, from 1814 until he died in 1873. You can visit his study, library, the living rooms, the wedding bedroom and the bedroom where he died.

➕ H5 ✉ Via G. Morone 1 (Piazza Belgioioso), 20121 ☎ 02 8646 60403 🕐 Tue–Fri 10–6, Sat 2–6 🚇 Duomo 🚌 61; tram 1, 2 ♿ Good 🎟 Moderate

MUSEO TEATRALE ALLA SCALA

teatroallascala.org

The museum was founded in 1913 and has a superb collection of theatrical memorabilia. This ranges from ornate stage-curtains and antique musical instruments to costumes (including those for Maria Callas and Rudolf Nureyev) and the Sambon collection of paintings and ceramics. You can take a tour of the auditorium, too.

➕ G5 ✉ Largo Ghiringhelli 1, 20121 ☎ 02 8970 9022 🕐 Daily 9–5.30 🚇 Duomo, Cordusio 🚌 61, tram 1, 2 ♿ Good 🎟 Moderate

PALAZZO DELLA RAGIONE
palazzodellaragionefotografia.it
This splendid redbrick medieval building, with rounded arches and a ground-floor loggia dominates Piazza Mercanti. It was built in 1233 by the *podestà* (governor) and now hosts photographic art shows.

➕ G6 ✉ Piazza Mercanti, 20123 ⏱ Tue–Sun 9.30–8.30, Thu, Sat until 10.30pm 🚇 Duomo 🚋 Tram 2, 3, 15, 24

PALAZZO MARINO
On the same square as the Teatro alla Scala, this is an imposing baroque palace with a late-19th-century facade. It was built in 1558 for Tommaso Marino, a wealthy Genoese financier, and since 1860 it has been the city's town hall. The palace is not open to the public, but don't miss the porticoed Courtyard of Honor, which can be glimpsed from Via Marina.

➕ H5 ✉ Piazza della Scala, 20121 👁 View from outside only 🚇 Duomo, Cordusio 🚋 61; tram 1, 2

PIAZZA MERCANTI
One of Milan's most historic squares, traffic-free Piazza Mercanti is home to the Palazzo della Ragione (▷ above), the Palazzo dei Giureconsulti and lovely marble Loggia degli Osii opposite. It's a pleasant spot for browsing, lunching alfresco or taking a breather.

➕ G6 ✉ Piazza Mercanti, 20121 🚇 Duomo 🚋 Tram 2, 3, 14, 15, 24

SAN FEDELE
sanfedele.net
This 16th-century Jesuit church, designed by Pellegrino Tibaldi, is one of the city's finest examples of baroque architecture. The elaborate facade is decorated with reliefs on the pediment and sculpted figures in the niches. Although internally less exciting, the church has some beautifully carved wooden furniture.

➕ H5 ✉ Piazza San Fedele, 20121 ☎ 02 8635 2215 ⏱ Mon, Wed–Thu 10–1 🚇 Duomo 🚋 61; tram 1, 2 ♿ Poor; 7 steps up to church 🎫 Free

VIA DANTE
Linking Largo Cairoli to Castello Sforzesco, this busy pedestrian thoroughfare, named after the Florentine poet Dante Alighieri, was built at the end of the 19th century. Alfresco cafés spill out onto the street, and elegant shops occupy the lower floors of fine neoclassical buildings. The northwest end of the street is dominated by an equestrian statue of Garibaldi and beyond it is the soaring clock tower of the Castello.

➕ G5 ✉ 20121 🚇 Cordusio, Cairoli 🚋 18, 50, 58; tram 19, 24 and others

Interior of San Fedele

City Highlights

This stroll through the heart of Milan will introduce you to some of the city's most famous landmarks.

DISTANCE: 2km (1.25 miles) **ALLOW:** 2 hours plus stops

START

PIAZZA DEL DUOMO
🚇 H6 🚇 Duomo

1 Start at the Piazza del Duomo, dominated by the west front of the Duomo (▷ 44–45). Walk along the right side of the cathedral and turn right down the narrow Via del Palazzo Reale.

2 Pass between Palazzo Reale (▷ 50) and Palazzo Arcivescovile. Go round the back of the latter via the bell tower and the rotunda. Turn left at the end of Via delle Ore.

3 Enter Piazza Fontana, with the 1783 fountain by Piermarini. Look behind it for a fine view of the Duomo and then return to the Piazza del Duomo.

4 Turn right through Galleria Vittorio (▷ 48–49) into Piazza della Scala. Cross in front of the Palazzo Marino and turn right. Take another right behind the *palazzo*.

END

PIAZZA DEL DUOMO
🚇 H6 🚇 Duomo

8 Passing in front of La Scala, follow Via Santa Margherita down to Piazza Mercanti, into Via Mercanti, which leads back to the Duomo.

7 Now in Piazza Belgioioso you can find Manzoni's house, now the Museo Manzoniano (▷ 54). Continue to Via Manzoni, where Museo Poldi Pezzoli (▷ 28) is on the right. Turn left back into Piazza della Scala, with the opera house, La Scala (▷ 53), on your right.

6 Here, too, is the statue of writer Manzoni. Leaving the piazza the way you entered, walk alongside the church. You will see Casa degli Omenoni ahead on the left, once home to the sculptor Leone Leoni.

5 This brings you into the Piazza San Fedele, with its baroque church.

Shopping

ANDREW'S TIES

adties.com

Italian ties made of wool, silk and cashmere in every imaginable shade and design. Shirts and sweaters as well.

H5 ⊠ Via Agnello 1, 20121
☎ 02 8646 1694 ⓖ Duomo

BORSALINO

borsalino.com

This internationally renowned milliners was founded in Milan, and is one of the world's oldest. Come to the atmospheric shop to browse the superb collection of hats in every shape and color for every occasion.

H5 ⊠ Galleria Vittorio Emanuele II, 20121
☎ 02 8901 5436 ⓖ Duomo

BRIAN & BARRY

thebrianebarrybuilding.it

There are 12 floors of affordable fashion and accessories at this striking department store, which offers an excellent range with good prices.

J5 ⊠ Via Durini 28, 20122 ☎ 02 9285 3547 ⓖ San Babila

FOOTBALL TEAM DUOMO

footballteam-eshop.it

Deck yourself in the colors of Milan's football favorites at the Juventus Corner, their official gear and sportswear section in this mega football-fan emporium. Or pick up a shirt, flag or hat emblazoned with the national team insignia.

H6 ⊠ Piazza del Duomo 20, 20122
☎ 02 8905 2922 ⓖ Duomo

FOR PETS ONLY

forpetsonly.it

For dogs who yearn to look every bit as chic as their owner; clothes, leads, baskets and lots more in the latest styles and fashions.

G5 ⊠ Via S. Pietro all'Orto 3, 20121
☎ 02 795 694 ⓖ San Babila

FURLA

furla.com

Chic leather bags and belts in high-fashion, minimalist designs, but with an original twist. Also scarves and shoes. Affordable prices.

H5 ⊠ Piazza del Duomo 31, 20122
☎ 02 8909 6782 ⓖ Duomo

GIOVANNI GALLI

giovannigalli.com

The shop for those who love all things sweet. The *marrons glacés* are legendary, and the traditional sweets and biscuits are good, too. There's another branch in Via Victor Hugo.

H7 ⊠ Corso di Porta Romana 2, 20122
☎ 02 8645 3112 ⓖ Missori

LIBRERIA HOEPLI

hoepli.it

Established in 1870, this bookshop, extending over six floors, has the most extensive stock in Milan of books in any language, on any subject.

H5 ⊠ Via Hoepli 5, 20121 ☎ 02 864 871
ⓖ Duomo

LIU.JO

liujo.it

This Italian designer features young, sharp styling, using a great range of fabrics to produce a collection that's a little different. Prices are mid-range, ensuring a good look at a good price.

J5 ⊠ Corso Vittorio Emanuele 30, 20122
☎ 02 7631 7658 ⓖ San Babila

PECK STOPPANI

peck.it

Milan's most prestigious delicatessen, with numerous stalls specializing in

bread, cheese, seafood, salami, marinated vegetables and other delights. The online shop will ship many products anywhere in the world.

➕ G6 ✉ Via Spadari 9, 20123 ☎ 02 802 3161 🚇 Duomo

PRADA

prada.com

This flagship menswear store of one of Milan's most famous labels carries everything you need to achieve that "Prada look". Treat yourself to some of the stylish accessories.

➕ H5 ✉ Galleria Vittorio Emanuele II 63, 20121 ☎ 02 876 979 🚇 Duomo

LA RINASCENTE

larinascente.it

Department stores are still rather alien to most Italians and Milan has only a handful. The best is La Rinascente, a monumental shop opposite the Duomo. It stretches over six floors and sells almost everything you could possibly want.

➕ H5 ✉ Piazza del Duomo, 20121 ☎ 02 88521 🚇 Duomo

Entertainment and Nightlife

LE BANQUE

lebanque.it

A popular nightspot in a former bank. A range of music fills the dance floor, which was once the bank's vault. Happy hour with an inclusive buffet is nightly from 6.30.

➕ G5 ✉ Via B. Porrone 6, 20121 ☎ 02 8669 6565 🚇 Cordusio

CINEMA ODEON 5

A huge mainstream cinema in the middle of Milan showing the latest American blockbusters, many in their original language. This 10-screen complex has good access for visitors with disabilities.

➕ H5 ✉ Via Santa Radegonda 8, 20121 ☎ 02 892 111 🚇 Duomo

TEATRO ALLA SCALA

teatroallascala.org

Opera, classical and the occasional musical boom out from Milan's, and possibly the world's, most prestigious playhouse (▷ 53). It's not just famous names at La Scala; Maria Callas was unknown when she made her debut here. The venue has a bar, museum, visitor area and an excellent bookshop with many titles in English. You can book a tour that takes in the fabulous gilded royal box, the stage and backstage areas.

➕ H5 ✉ Piazza della Scala, 20121 ☎ 02 7200 3744 🚇 Duomo/Cordusio

TEATRO NUOVO

teatronuovo.it

All types of plays are staged here, including some excellent comedy, musicals and dance productions. There is capacity for more than 1,000 people, who come to see performances by some of the famous actors who appear here on a regular basis.

➕ J5 ✉ Piazza San Babila, 20121 ☎ 02 794 026 🚇 San Babila

Where to Eat

<table>
<tr><td colspan="2">PRICES</td></tr>
<tr><td colspan="2">Prices are approximate, based on a 3-course meal for one person.</td></tr>
<tr><td>€€€</td><td>over €55</td></tr>
<tr><td>€€</td><td>€25–€55</td></tr>
<tr><td>€</td><td>under €25</td></tr>
</table>

BOEUCC (€€€)

boeucc.it

It's worth splashing out for a special occasion here, Milan's oldest restaurant, which opened in 1696. Stone fluted pillars, oriental rugs and soft lights provide an elegant setting to enjoy excellent Milanese cooking. Or you can choose to eat in the garden in fine weather.

🔡 H5 ✉ Piazza Belgioioso 2, 20121 ☎ 02 7602 0224 🕔 Mon–Fri lunch, dinner; Sun dinner only 🚇 Duomo

CAFFÈ MERCANTI (€)

At this café/bar, seating is either in the upper balcony area, with mirrors and chandeliers, or outside under canopies with heaters. Good snacks such as *panini* and salads.

🔡 G6 ✉ Via dei Mercanti 21, 20123 ☎ 02 7208 0394 🕔 Daily 6am–1am 🚇 Cordusio

CAMPARINO IN GALLERIA (€€)

camparino.it

Famous Milan bar, owned by the Miani family, with an outside terrace ideally placed for people-watching. Prepare to pay a high price for your Negroni or Campari Americano

🔡 H6 ✉ Galleria Vittorio Emanuele II/Piazza del Duomo 21, 20121 ☎ 02 8646 4435 🕔 Tue–Sun. Closed Aug 🚇 Duomo

CHARLESTON (€)

ristorantecharleston.it

In the heart of the shopping area, serving a wide variety of pizza plus some interesting Florentine dishes. Dine under the gazebo in summer.

🔡 H5 ✉ Piazza del Liberty 8, 20121 ☎ 02 798 631 🕔 Daily 🚇 Duomo, San Babila

CRACCO (€€€)

ristorantecracco.it

Modern Italian cuisine cooked with the finest and freshest ingredients have given Carlo Cracco's restaurant an international reputation. Reservations advised.

🔡 H5 ✉ Corso Vittorio Emanuele II, 20121 ☎ 02 876 774 🕔 Mon–Fri lunch, dinner; Sat dinner only. Closed 2 weeks Aug 🚇 Duomo

DI GENNARO (€)

di-gennaro.it

Not far from the Duomo and good for an after-show meal, this pizzeria and restaurant has been producing classics from the old-fashioned tiled oven for many years.

🔡 H5 ✉ Via Santa Radegonda 14, 20121 ☎ 02 805 3454 🕔 Fri–Wed all day 🚇 Duomo

GB BAR (€€)

An excellent pit-stop if you've been sightseeing in the Duomo area, this friendly bar offers a huge range of great value panini (sandwiches). All the

---

A PLETHORA OF PIZZA

There's pizza and there's pizza, and you'll find some of the best in Milan. Seek out the pizzerias where the food is cooked in wood-fired ovens (*forno a legna*). The pizzas are usually thin crust and made from age-old recipes, and the best ones are normally prepared by one of the many Neapolitan chefs working in the city. A true Italian pizza does not include exotic toppings such as pineapple or corn.

cheese and ham classics are on offer, alongside gourmet choices such as smoked swordfish, pulled pork or mushroom with truffle.

🚩 H5 ✉ Via Agnello18, 20121 ☎ 02 863 446 🕐 Daily 7–6.30 🚇 Duomo

IL GABBIANO (€)

Near the Duomo, this *gelateria* sells milkshakes and fruit salad as well as a large selection of ice cream and sorbets. You can also sit outside.

🚩 H5 ✉ Via Ugo Foscolo 3, 20121 ☎ 02 7202 2411 🕐 Daily 🚇 Duomo

MARCHESI (€)

pasticceriamarchesi.com

Enjoy the pastries, tarts, salads and much more at this Milan institution. Take away some sweets, cakes or chocolates—the gift-wrapping is a joy.

🚩 F5 ✉ Via Santa Maria alla Porta 11a, 20123 ☎ 02 876 730 🕐 Mon–Sat 7.30am–8pm, Sun 8.30–1 🚇 Cordusio, Cairoli

SAVINI (€€€)

savanimilano.it

Legendary restaurant that has been serving meals since 1867, especially to the rich and famous. The well-prepared food, based on the finest ingredients, lives up to the best Milanese traditions, and this is the most stylish place in Milan to be seen. You'll probably need to have your concierge make your dinner reservation.

🚩 H5 ✉ Galleria Vittorio Emanuele II, 20121 ☎ 02 7200 3433 🕐 Daily lunch, dinner. Closed 3 weeks Aug 🚇 Duomo

T'A MILANO (€€)

tamilano.com

Fabulous chocolates and pastries are on offer in this famous *pasticceria*, run by the Alemagna family, but walk through

and you'll come to the bar and bistro, serving drinks and food all day. The surroundings are a joy, with marble floors, velvet banquettes and gleaming chandeliers, with food and service to match.

🚩 G6 ✉ Via Clerici 1, 20121 ☎ 02 8738 6130 🕐 Mon–Fri lunch, dinner 🚇 Duomo

TRATTORIA MILANESE (€)

For a taste of old Milan, come to this tiny trattoria in the heart of the city. In business for a century, the trattoria reflects the past and the excellent food lives up to the Milanese tradition. The menu is filled with old favorites, prepared without any *nuovo* frills: polenta, excellent gnocchi and risottos.

🚩 G6 ✉ Via Santa Marta 11, 20123 ☎ 02 8645 1991 🕐 Wed–Mon lunch, dinner. Closed mid-Jul to Aug 🚇 Cordusio, Missori

VICTORIA RISTORANTE (€€)

victoriaristorante.it

Discreet café behind the Piazza della Scala; the perfect spot for a pizza or pasta lunch, an early-evening drink or a nightcap. The menu offers creative takes on regional dishes, and a specialty is the impeccably fresh tuna tartare. You may spot artistes from La Scala at the next table.

🚩 G5 ✉ Via Clerici 1, 20121 ☎ 02 869 0792 🕐 Daily 🚇 Duomo

MILANESE COOKING

Dishes that appear on most menus include the *risotto allo zafferano* (rice cooked with saffron), minestrone soup, polenta *pasticciata* (polenta pie with cheese sauce and white truffles), *costoletta alla milanese* (breaded veal cutlet), *osso buco alla milanese* (veal stewed with the marrow bone) and *rostin negàa* (veal chops in white wine).

The Northwest

This attractive quarter of Milan is dominated by Parco Sempione and the austere Castello Sforzesco. In complete contrast, the bohemian Brera offers medieval streets, restaurants and bars.

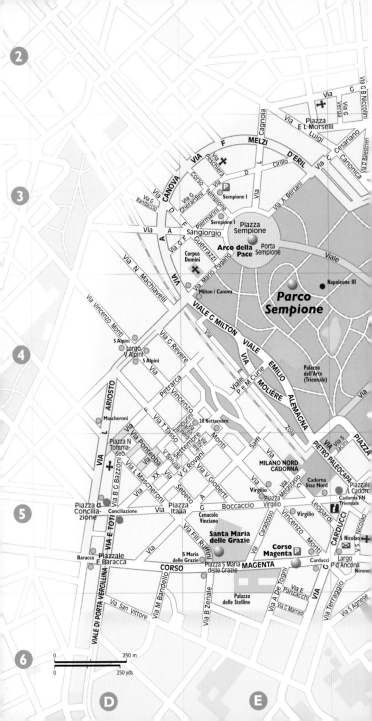

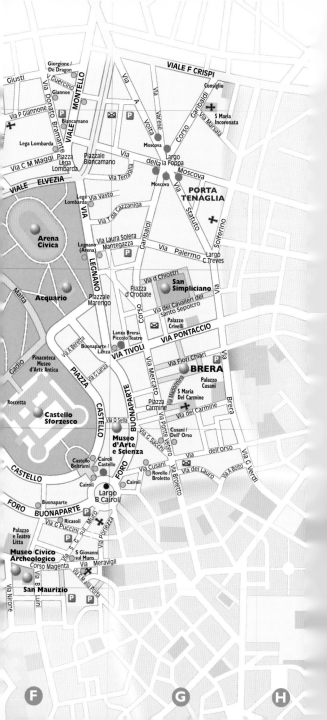

Arco della Pace

TOP 25

Triumphal detail from the impressive Arco della Pace at the north end of Parco Sempione

THE BASICS

✠ E3

✉ Piazza Sempione, 20154 and 20145

🚌 57, 61; tram 1, 30

♿ Good

HIGHLIGHTS

● The huge bronze Chariot of Peace (25m/82ft high)
● A distant view from the Parco Sempione
● The initial impact as you approach from Corso Sempione

Milan's triumphal arch was intended as a monument to Napoleon's victories. With his fall from power in 1814, the project came to a standstill and he was never to see its completion.

Napoleon's dream The Arch of Victories, as it was at first known, was finished in 1838 under the Austrian Emperor, Ferdinand I. In commemoration of the European Peace Treaty of 1815 he changed the name to the Arch of Peace (Arco della Pace) and made changes to the bas-reliefs. The formal monument marks the northwest end of the Parco Sempione, and the start of the Corso Sempione, Napoleon's highway to the Simplon Pass.

Monumental construction The arch was designed by Luigi Cagnola and inspired by the arch of Septimius Severus in the Forum in Rome. Work began in 1807, halted in 1814, and resumed in 1826 under Ferdinand I of Austria. The circular piazza around it was redesigned in the 1980s and closed to traffic. The arch is best seen from a distance, preferably from the park side, where you can see the Chariot of Peace on the top of the monument. A face-lift has returned the arch to its former glory and the marble gleams once again.

Beyond the arch The two buildings either side of the arch on the park side were toll houses. Open-air concerts are held in the circular piazza on summer evenings, but avoid after dark.

Castello Sforzesco

From left: tourist entrance; Rondanini Pietà; outer wall of the Castello Sforzesco

The castle is a vast brick quadrilateral, dominated on the town side by the Filarete Tower. It stands as a symbol of the golden Renaissance age, and today is home to the excellent civic museums.

Through the centuries Built as a fortress by the Visconti family between 1358 and 1368, the castle was all but demolished after their downfall. It was transformed into a Renaissance fort under Francesco Sforza, and his son, who became Duke of Milan, and turned into a sumptuous residence. By the early 19th century, Napoleon had turned what was left of the building into soldiers' quarters. In 1884, the city planned to demolish the castle, but architect Luca Beltrami transformed it into a museum.

Exploring the museums Start your visit at the entrance under the Filarete Tower. Beyond the Piazza d'Armi is the Renaissance Corte Ducale, residence of the Sforzas, and now home to the collections. Michelangelo's Rondanini Pietà is in a separate space, created as part of the ongoing upgrade of the museum. On the upper floor is the furniture collection and art gallery, whose Italian Renaissance masterpieces include works by Mantegna, Giovanni Bellini, Antonello da Messina and Filippo Lippi, as well as Lombard artists. The first and second floors are devoted to the applied arts, with a collection of musical instruments and the rare Trivulzio Tapestries, designed by Bramantino. The basement houses the archaeology museum.

HIGHLIGHTS

- Mausoleum of Bernabò Visconti (1363), Bonino da Campione
- Sala delle Asse (Room 8), with fresco decoration attributed to da Vinci
- Sala degli Scarlioni (Room 15): Michelangelo's *Rondanini Pietà* (1552–64) and Gaston de Foix's funerary monument, *Agostino Busti*

TIP

- Lots to see—visit the museums on a wet day, the grounds on a sunny one.

Corso Magenta

From left: a tram on Corso Magenta; Caffè Litta; imposing facade of Palazzo Litta

THE BASICS

🗺 E5

✉ Extending east from Porta Magenta to the junction with Via Meravigli

🍴 Numerous cafés and restaurants

Ⓜ Conciliazione, Cadorna

🚌 18, 67; tram 16, 19

HIGHLIGHTS

● Santa Maria delle Grazie and Leonardo da Vinci's *The Last Supper* (*c.*1495–97) (▷ 72–73)
● Museo Civico Archeologico (▷ 68–69)
● San Maurizio (▷ 71)
● Bar Magenta—historic café (▷ 77)

Any visit to Milan should include this *corso*, one of Milan's most elegant streets flanked by historic *palazzi* and home to Leonardo da Vinci's *The Last Supper* at the Church of Santa Maria delle Grazie.

Along the old road The oldest trace of civilization here is the Roman tower in the grounds of the Archaeological Museum (▷ 68–69), the only surviving above-ground section of the city's Roman walls. On the same site are the ruins of the ancient Benedictine Maggiore monastery, founded in the ninth century and renovated in the early 1500s. The rest of the Corso is more recent, typified by baroque, neoclassical and 19th-century mansions.

Plenty to see This is one of Milan's most affluent districts, with chic boutiques, antiques shops and historic buildings. The great magnet is the Church of Santa Maria delle Grazie, whose splendid terra-cotta bulk dominates. The piazza is normally milling with visitors, awaiting their alloted 15-minute slot for da Vinci's *The Last Supper* in the refectory adjoining the church. Going east, the Palazzo delle Stelline at No. 59, a school for orphans in the 17th century, has been transformed into a conference facility and hotel. Beyond the crossroads is the large baroque facade of Palazzo Litta (No. 24), now home to the Teatro Litta (▷ 77), and across the road, beyond the Archaeological Museum, the Church of San Maurizio (No. 15, ▷ 71) is full of 16th-century frescoes.

24

FERROVIE DELLO STATO

S. p. A.

Museo Civico Archeologico

HIGHLIGHTS

● Coppa Trivulzio
● Parabiago Plate
● The torso of Hercules: discovered among ruins of Roman baths on what is now Corso Europa
● *Portrait of Maximin* (mid-3rd-century AD): one of a series of portraits dating from the Roman era

Milan was once a powerful Roman city, and this museum, in the ruins of the Benedictine Maggiore monastery, exhibits some fine examples of Roman sculpture and everyday items.

Moving collections The exhibits were once housed in the Castello Sforzesco, in the city's archaeological and numismatic collections. Following World War II, several sections were transferred here, next to the church of San Maurizio, with some remaining in the Castello. The monastery, once the largest women's convent in Milan, was built in the ninth century, rebuilt in the 16th, and badly bombed in 1943.

Roman and other finds Fragments of Roman funerary stones, sarcophagi and capitals are

From far left: ancient Bronze Age stone menhir with engraving; detail of a relief on a Roman stone wall; the entrance to the museum

arranged around the cloister at the front of the museum, with pride of place going to the Masso di Bornio, a large stone whose carvings date back to the third millennium BC. Inside, a model of Roman Milan (Mediolanum) introduces the Roman collection. The basement is devoted to Greek and Etruscan exhibits and a tiny section to works of art from Gandhara (what is now northern Pakistan and Afghanistan). Take a look at the Coppa Trivulzio in the Roman section, which is behind the black screen and quite easy to miss. It is an exquisite late fourth-century goblet in emerald-green glass, carved from a single piece of glass. The Roman Parabiago Plate is a large silver-gilt, embossed patera (weighing 3.5kg/8lb) discovered in 1907, from Parabiago, northwest of Milan.

THE BASICS

museoarcheologicomilano.it

✚ F5

✉ Corso Magenta 15, 20123

☎ 02 8844 5208

🕐 Tue–Sun 9–5.30. Closed 1 Jan, 1 May, 25 Dec

🚇 Cadorna, Cairoli

🚌 50, 58, 94; tram 16, 19

♿ Poor; phone ahead (tel 02 8846 5720)

💶 Inexpensive

ℹ Small booklets in English, inexpensive

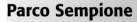

Parco Sempione

TOP 25

Cool and inviting, particularly in summer, the park is popular with locals and visitors

THE BASICS

+ E4

✉ Piazza Castello–Piazza Sempione, (8 entrances around perimeter), 20154

☎ 02 8846 7383

🕐 Park: daily 6.30am–8/9/10/11.30pm depending on season.
Torre Branca: Tue 3–7pm, Wed 10.30–12.30, 3–7, Thu, Fri 8.30–7, 8.30pm–12am, Sat, Sun 10.30–2, 2.30–7, Sun also 8.30pm–12am; winter hours are shorter; check website (museobranca.it) for details. Closed in bad weather

🍴 Cafés in park

🚇 Cadorna, Cairioli, Lanza, Moscova

🚌 43, 57, 61, 94; tram 1, 4, 27

♿ Park free; Torre Branca moderate, over 60s and children under 3 free

HIGHLIGHTS

● Arena Civica
● Torre Branca
● *Bagni Misteriosi*, sculpture by Giorgio de Chirico, found behind the Palazzo dell'Arte
● View of Arco della Pace from the lake

A welcome break from the city noise, with a fine view of the Castello Sforzesco, the Parco Sempione was once part of the vast hunting ground of the Sforza family, who occupied the castle. It became a public park in the late 19th century.

Early uses In the early 1800s the French used the land as an exercise ground for their armed forces. Napoleon planned to build a great piazza around the castle and turn the area into the new heart of the city, but apart from the Arco della Pace (▷ 64) and the Arena Civica (▷ 74) the plans never materialized. The 47ha (116-acre) public park was begun in 1893 when Emilio Alemagna landscaped the area on the lines of an English park—as was the fashion.

The country in town The gardens stretch from the castle to the Arco della Pace—a landscape of lawns, large trees, winding paths and a lake with a small bridge. On the west side, you can't miss the Torre Branca, a steel tower with a lift that will take you to the top for the best views over the city. Designer Roberto Cavalli has opened a restaurant at the base of the tower (▷ 78). The nearby Palazzo dell'Arte, built in 1933, is the permanent site of the Triennale Decorative Arts Exhibition. The park is dotted with modern sculpture and monuments, has lots to amuse children, including sailing boats on the lake, and there's entertainment in the summer months. Although the park is open late into the evening, it is best avoided after dark.

San Maurizio

The unremarkable gray baroque facade of this church on the busy Corso Magenta gives no hint of the glorious interior. Step inside and you are greeted by a riot of beautiful baroque frescoes, decorating every surface.

Important convent The church was built in 1503 for the adjoining Monastero Maggiore, formerly one of the most prestigious monasteries in Milan, and home to Benedictine nuns. The monastery was largely destroyed in the 19th century but is today the site of the Museo Civico Archeologico (▷ 68–69).

Church meets state The church was constructed in two main parts: one hall for the congregation and a larger cloistered hall for the nuns. The two were separated by a partition wall and altar, which face you as you go into the church. The nuns were able to participate in Eucharists celebrated in the public hall through the little doors, which you can see in the arch in the central fresco to the left of the altar; they could also receive Communion through the tiny opening (the *comunichino*) on the right of the altar below the figure of Christ.

Wonderful frescoes On both sides of the partition wall is the *Passion of Christ*. Many of the frescoes were executed by Bernardino Luini (*c.* 1480–1532), one of the most prominent followers of Leonardo da Vinci; the chapels on the left were decorated by his pupils.

THE BASICS

✚ F5
✉ Corso Magenta 15, 20123
🕐 Tue–Sat 9–7.30 (can sometimes close for no reason); closed 1 Jan, 1 May, 25 Dec
🚇 Cadorna
🚌 50, 59; tram 19, 20, 24
♿ Poor
🎟 Free
ℹ Guidebooks in Italian only

HIGHLIGHTS

● Frescoes by Bernardino Luini, including *Life of St. Catherine*
● *The Adoration of the Magi*, Antonio Campi
● Frescoes by unattributed artists
● Classical concerts in the nuns' hall in winter
● Excellent lighting to view the frescoes in detail

Santa Maria delle Grazie

HIGHLIGHTS

● *The Last Supper*, Leonardo da Vinci (in the adjoining Refectory)
● The Bramante Cloister
● Chapel of St. Corona, with frescoes by Gaudenzio Ferrari
● Madonna delle Grazie Chapel
● *Madonna delle Grazie delivering Milan from the Plague*, Il Cerano

TIPS

● It is not possible to view *The Last Supper* without reserving ahead.
● Guided city tours may include entrance to *The Last Supper* if you can't get tickets.

While *The Last Supper* is a real highlight, the church itself should not be missed. Although it was built over a mere 26 years, it gives the impression of being two completely different churches.

Renaissance gem Guiniforte Solari designed the church for the Dominican Order in 1463–90. The contrast of styles between the Dominican late-Gothic nave, with its wealth of decoration, and the pure, harmonious domed apse built by Bramante marks the rapid change that came with the Renaissance. In 1943, a bomb destroyed the cloister, but, miraculously, *The Last Supper* and the dome, survived.

Glorious architecture The magnificent brick and terra-cotta exterior, crowned by Bramante's

Clockwise from top far left: detail from Leonardo da Vinci's The Last Supper; *overall view of the church; detail of the arches at the top of the dome*

grand dome, is best seen from Corso Magenta. From the Renaissance portal, you enter Solari's nave, with its richly decorated arches and vaults. The Bramante Cloister, surrounding a garden, is familiarly known as Chiostrino delle Rane after the bronze frogs *(rane)* at the fountain. During services you can reach it via the street entrance on Via Caradosso.

Da Vinci's masterpiece Ludovico Il Moro commissioned this fresco in the refectory adjoining the church in 1494. It is one of the most famous in the world, but the experimental techniques used by da Vinci led to signs of deterioration within 20 years of its completion. Much restoration has been done to return the painting to its former glory. Booking in advance is compulsory.

THE BASICS

cenacolovinciano.net

✚ E5

✉ Piazza Santa Maria delle Grazie, 20123

☎ 02 467 6111

🕐 Basilica Mon–Sat 7–12, 3–7.15, Sun and holidays 7.30–12.30, 3.30–8.45. *The Last Supper* Tue–Sun 8.15–6.45

🚇 Conciliazione, Cardorna

♿ Good; 3 steps

🎟 Church free. *The Last Supper* expensive

❓ Book as early as possible to view *The Last Supper*. Tickets must be picked up 20 min in advance of admission time ☎ Reservations 02 9280 0360

More to See

ACQUARIO
acquariocivicomilano.eu

Set in a fine art nouveau building, this excellent aquarium was completed in March 2006. It houses some 150 different species from marine and freshwater environments. The transparent bridge lets you look at the fish from all angles.

🔸 F4 🖂 Via Gadio 2, 20121 ☎ 02 8846 5750 🕐 Tue–Sun 9–5.30 🚇 Lanza 🚌 57; tram 3, 4, 7, 12 ♿ Good 💷 Inexpensive

ARENA CIVICA
This huge amphitheater was built in 1806 to seat 30,000 spectators. It has hosted soccer games and pop concerts; today it is mainly used for athletic events.

🔸 F3 🖂 Viale Giorgio Byron 2, Parco Sempione, 20154 🕐 Open for events only 🚇 Lanza 🚌 57, 70; tram 3, 4, 12, 14

BRERA DISTRICT
The Brera is one of the oldest and most attractive districts in Milan. For many years it was inhabited by artists and there is still a hint of Bohemia. Via Brera is its liveliest street, popular for its open-air cafés, inviting *trattorie*, galleries, street vendors and late-night bars.

🔸 G4 🖂 20121 🚌 61; tram 1, 27

MUSEO D'ARTE E SCIENZA
museoartescienza.com

This private museum, near the castle, shows you how to tell the difference between genuine and fake antiques—2,000 of them.

🔸 G4 🖂 Via Q. Sella 4, 20121 ☎ 02 7202 2488 🕐 Mon–Fri 10–6 🚇 Cairoli, Lanza 🚌 57, 61; tram 3, 4, 12, 14 ♿ None 💷 Free/donation; guided tours expensive

SAN SIMPLICIANO
sansimpliciano.it

This handsome basilica is the finest of the churches in the Brera quarter. It was founded in the fourth century, possibly by Sant'Ambrogio, and reconstructed in the 12th century.

🔸 G4 🖂 Piazza San Simpliciano 7, 20121 ☎ 02 862 274 🕐 Mon–Fri 9–12, 2.15–7, Sat–Sun 9.30–7 🚇 Lanza 🚌 57, 61; tram 12, 14 ♿ Good 💷 Free

Down the Via Brera in a Milanese tram

Some Milanese Treasures

This gentle walk takes you from the castle via one of the finest churches in the city to the park and into the bohemian Brera district.

DISTANCE: 3.5km (2.2 miles) **ALLOW:** Half a day with stops

START

CASTELLO SFORZESCO
🚇 F4 🚊 Cairoli

❶ Start at the clock tower of the Castello Sforzesco (▷ 65). With your back to the castle, follow the path around to the right and cross over the main road into Via Minghetti.

❷ At the end, cross Piazzale Codorna past the station into Via Carducci. Continue until you meet Corso Magenta (▷ 66–67). Go right and follow the road to Santa Maria delle Grazie (▷ 72–73).

❸ The adjoining refectory contains da Vinci's famous *The Last Supper* (▷ 72). Across the piazza, just past the church, turn into Via Ruffini.

❹ Turn right into Piazza Italia. Cross over and go right into Via Saffi. At the end turn left and continue round into Viale P. e M. Curie and over the railway line.

END

BRERA DISTRICT
🚇 G4 🚊 Lanza

❽ Take the second left into Via Erbe. Cross over Via Mercato and you are in the heart of the Brera district, a perfect spot for lunch.

❼ Turning right inside the park takes you back to the castle; left takes you to the triumphal Arco della Pace (▷ 64). At the east side of the park is the Arena Civica (▷ 74) and the Acquario (▷ 74). Exit near here onto Via Gadio and cross into Foro Buonaparte.

❻ Enter through the gate between the Palazzo dell'Arte (▷ 70) and the Eiffel Tower–like building the Torre Branca (▷ 70), and this will bring you into the main body of the park.

❺ At the end, cross the road to enter Parco Sempione (▷ 70) opposite.

Shopping

10 CORSO COMO

10corsocomo.com

For sheer style don't miss this fabulous store on the fashionable Corso Como. A stunning array of men's and women's fashions, accessories, homewares, books and CDs and something for the little ones, too. Restaurant, B&B and library on the premises as well.

⊞ G2 ✉ Corso Como 10, 20154 ☎ 02 2900 2674 🚇 Garibaldi

ATRIBU

See or buy the works of young designers before they become household names.

⊞ G4 ✉ Corso Giuseppe Garibaldi 49, 20124 ☎ 02 867 127 🚇 Lanza

BUSCEMI DISCHI

buscemidischi.it

One of the city's oldest and most famous record stores, split between two shops.

⊞ F5 ✉ Corso Magenta 31, 20123 ☎ 02 804 103 🚇 Cadorna

CARTOLERIA RUFFINI

See the craftsmen at work out the back producing handmade notebooks, albums, boxes and letter racks, which are then sold at the front of this traditional old shop.

⊞ E5 ✉ Via F. Ruffini 1, 20123 ☎ 02 463 074 🚇 Conciliazione

DIEGO DALLA PALMA

diegodallapalma.com

Lipsticks, powders and paints from this household name among Italy's make-up elite. Knowledgeable staff can advise you on the products to use to suit your skin tone.

⊞ G4 ✉ Via Madonnina 15, 20121 ☎ 02 876 818 🚇 Lanza

E.E. ERCOLESSI

ercolessi.gpa.it

Large wooden cabinets hold the extensive range of pens ranging from familiar brands to limited editions, and the company's marble-green signature pen.

⊞ E5 ✉ Corso Magenta 25, 20123 ☎ 02 8645 4154 🚇 Cadorna

LA FUNGHERIA

lafungheria.com

To the west of Corso Magenta you will find quality mushrooms and truffles in this shop. It's worth the little extra journey to get that slightly more unusual gift to take home.

⊞ B5 ✉ Via Marghera 14, 20149 ☎ 02 439 0089 🚇 Wagner, De Angeli

LUISA BECCARIA

luisabeccaria.it

Delicate satin and chiffon feature in this designer's dreamy, feminine styles.

⊞ G4 ✉ Via Formentini 1, 20121 ☎ 02 801 417 🚇 Lanza

MERCATO D'ANTIQUARIATO DI BRERA

Don't miss this monthly antiques market of about 60 stalls laden with collectibles at bargain prices.

⊞ G4 ✉ Via Fiori Chiari, 20121 🕐 3rd Sun of month 8.30–6 🚇 Lanza

IS IT ANTIQUE?

Bear in mind that under Italian law an antique need only be made of old materials. For this reason, what would be called reproduction elsewhere is quite legally called an antique in Italy. Hundreds of shops all over Milan sell these antiques, but the narrow, cobbled lanes of the Brera district and the canal area are particularly pleasant places to browse.

Entertainment and Nightlife

BAR MAGENTA

Friendly staff, wooden tables and a top shelf stacked full of the world's finest spirits. Every type of music from jazz to rock and punk is played on the bar's stereo system. Popular with students and fans of sport—particularly Italian football—so it can get noisy.

🔹 F5 ✉ Via G. Carducci 13, 20123 ☎ 02 8053 3808 🚇 Cordusio

CRT TEATRO DELL'ARTE

triennale.org

Most performances are in Italian but the passionate music and contemporary dance displays will need no translation. Several yearly dance festivals with top directors, dancers and actors.

🔹 E4 ✉ Viale E. Alemagna 6, 20121 ☎ 02 724 341 🚇 Cadorna

GLORIA MULTISALA

ucicinemas.it

This renovated cinema comprises two theaters, the Garbo and the Marilyn. Both have big screens and a good sound system. Bar.

🔹 D5 ✉ Corso Vercelli 18, 20144 ☎ 02 4800 8908 🚇 Pagano, Conciliazione

HOLLYWOOD

discotecahollywood.it

Getting in is neither cheap nor easy—you'll need lots of cash and your latest Galleria Emanuele outfit. But once inside you could be rubbing shoulders with Milan's beautiful people.

🔹 G2 ✉ Corso Como 15, 20154 ☎ 338 505 5761 🚇 Garibaldi

JAMAICA

jamaicabar.it

Since 1920, Brera's painters and artists have flocked to this legendary haunt, and it's still popular today. The cocktails are excellent, the wine well chosen, and you can eat any time throughout the day.

🔹 G4 ✉ Via Brera 32, 20121 ☎ 02 876 723 🚇 Montenapoleone

OLD FASHION CAFÉ

oldfashion.it

Exclusive nightspot in a former ballroom that attracts a chic crowd to its theme nights.

🔹 E4 ✉ Viale E. Alemagna 6, 20121 ☎ 02 805 6231 🚇 Cadorna

TEATRO DAL VERME

dalverme.org

The small theater has a full schedule of classical and semi-classical concerts and chamber music performed by touring groups and local musicians.

🔹 F5 ✉ Via San Giovanni sul Muro 2, 20121 ☎ 02 87905 🚇 Cairoli

TEATRO LITTA

teatrolitta.it

Children's plays make up the lion's share of performances in this theater, in the striking Palazzo Litta. The magic and dance displays will delight English-speaking kids, although the Italian drama shows may be beyond them. A peek inside the classic baroque theater is worth it for those interested in architecture.

🔹 F5 ✉ Corso Magenta 24, 20123 ☎ 02 805 5882 🚇 Cadorna

TOCQUEVILLE 13

tocqueville13.club

It may be named after the famous political thinker, but it's celebrity-spotting the punters come for on the club's ultracool party nights. Feast on tapas all night.

🔹 G2 ✉ Via A. de Tocqueville 13, 20154 ☎ 348 374 6374 🚇 Garibaldi

Where to Eat

PRICES
Prices are approximate, based on a 3-course meal for one person.
€€€ over €55
€€ €25–€55
€ under €25

ALICE RISTORANTE (€€–€€€)

aliceristorante.it

On the second floor of Eataly Milano Smeraldo, Alice is part of a complex that combines fine dining, a specialty grocery store and venue for food and cultural events.

➕ G2 ✉ Piazza XXV Aprile 10, 20121 ☎ 02 4949 7340 🕐 Mon–Sat 12–2, 7.30–10 🚇 Muscova, Garibaldi

BIFFI (€€)

biffipasticceria.it

Biffi has been around since the end of the 19th century and is the place to try their own *panettone*.

➕ D5 ✉ Corso Magenta 87, 20123 ☎ 02 4800 6702 🕐 Tue–Sun 🚇 Conciliazione

C'ERA UNA VOLTA (€€)

The atmosphere at this trattoria changes with the time of day: lunch is relaxed, loud and crowded with office workers; for dinner it's tablecloths, candles and couples. Good pasta and fish dishes.

➕ G3 ✉ Via Palermo 20, 20121 ☎ 02 654 060 🕐 Mon–Sat lunch, dinner 🚇 Moscova

CHOCOLAT (€)

chocolatmilano.it

Gelato in many shades of chocolate and other flavors as well. On a weekend you'll have to stand in line as this place is no secret.

➕ E5 ✉ Via Giovanni Boccaccio 9, 20123 ☎ 02 4810 0597 🕐 Daily to 1am 🚇 Cadorna

JUST CAVALLI CAFÉ (€€€)

milano.cavalliclub.com

Designer Roberto Cavalli's hot spot at the base of the Torre Branca. The semi-circular steel and glass structure encloses a sophisticated restaurant. Sip cocktails with celebrities and eat dishes from worldwide cuisines. Garden with a gazebo.

➕ E4 ✉ Viale Luigi Cameons, Torre Branca, 20121 ☎ 02 311 817 🕐 Mon–Sat dinner 🚇 Cadorna

L'OSTERIA DI BRERA (€€–€€€)

osteriadibrera.it

In one of the most picturesque streets in the Brera district, impeccably fresh seafood is stylishly presented amid white linens and crystal.

➕ G4 ✉ Via Fiori Chiari 8, 20121 ☎ 02 8909 6628 🕐 Daily noon–midnight 🚇 Cadorna

PASTICCERIA VILLA (€)

Established in 1896, this *pasticceria/restaurant*, where you can stand at the bar and buy cakes to take away, has a lovely outdoor area where you can enjoy cream cakes, desserts, pastries or a full meal. The daily lunch fixed menu is good value and imaginative.

➕ F5 ✉ Piazzale Cadorna 9, 20123 ☎ 02 8645 1178 🕐 Mon–Sat 🚇 Cadorna

ROCKING HORSE (€€)

This is a good, straightforward, typical Milanese trattoria, serving Milanese specialties such as risotto, *spaghetti alle cozze* (with mussels) and *cotoletta alla Milanese* (breaded veal escalope) alongside crisp *pizze* with imaginative toppings. It's usually busy with locals at lunch and dinner, always a good sign.

➕ G2 ✉ Corso Como 12, 20154 ☎ 02 657 0433 🕐 Daily lunch, dinner 🚇 Garibaldi

The Southwest

Probably not the most visited part of the city, this area features some of the most striking churches in Milan, medieval remains, quiet piazzas and the bohemian shopping street of Corso di Porto Ticinese.

Top 25

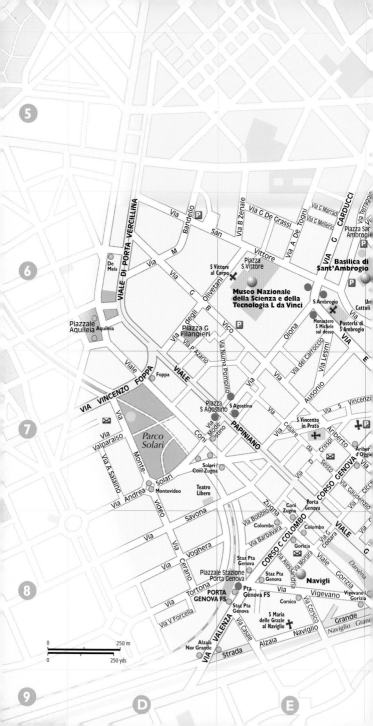

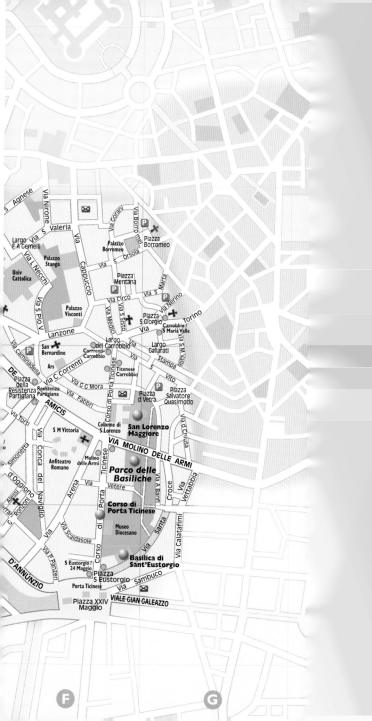

Basilica di Sant'Ambrogio

HIGHLIGHTS

● Sarcophagus of Stilicho
● 10th-century *ciborium* (canopy)
● Ninth-century altar front sculpted by Volvinio and encrusted with gems, gold and silver
● Chapel of San Vittore in Ciel d'Oro, with fifth-century dome mosaic
● Underground crypt with remains of saints Ambrogio, Gervasius and Protusius in a single urn

TIP

● There is an annual market on St. Ambrogio's day (7 December) with stalls around the church. Expect crowds.

Named for the patron saint of Milan, Sant'Ambrogio is a supreme example of Romanesque architecture and a prototype for 11th- and 12th-century churches all over Lombardy.

Years in the building The church, west of the Duomo, was originally built between AD379 and 386 by Bishop Ambrogio, who was later made patron saint of Milan. The church was enlarged in the ninth and 11th centuries, although Bramante's Portico della Canonica was left unfinished until the 17th century, and had to be reconstructed after the 1943 bombings.

Superb decoration This is one of the loveliest churches in the city. The fine redbrick exterior, with its two bell towers (ninth-century one to

The atrium of the Basilica of Sant'Ambrogio, one of Milan's finest churches

the right, 12th-century one to the left) is best seen from Piazza Sant'Ambrogio. Access to the church is via the lovely Ansperto atrium, which was built as a refuge for pilgrims. The church interior, simple and harmonious, has three aisles and distinctive ribbed cross vaulting. The apse is embellished with mosaics (sixth- to eighth-century, much restored) depicting Christ between Milanese saints and martyrs.

Not to be missed Beautifully carved in the fourth century, the Sarcophagus of Stilicho, below the pulpit and left of the nave, is traditionally believed to be the tomb of the Roman military commander Stilicho and his wife and is one of the few surviving features of the original church. The pulpit above it was constructed from 12th-century fragments.

THE BASICS

basilicasantambrogio.it

➕ F6

✉ Piazza Sant'Ambrogio 15, 20123

☎ 02 8645 0895

🕐 Mon–Sat 7.30–12.30, 2.30–7, Sun and festivals 7.30–1, 3–8. No visits during services

🚇 Sant'Ambrogio

🚌 50, 58, 94

♿ Good

✋ Free; Chapel of San Vittore in Ciel d'Oro inexpensive

Museo Nazionale della Scienza e della Tecnologia

TOP 25

HIGHLIGHTS

● The Leonardo Gallery
● Leonardo self-portrait
● Watchmaker's workshop (1750)
● Early steam locomotives
● The *Ebe*, a huge schooner
● The *Conte Biancamano*, a 1925 transatlantic liner with period furnishings
● Early computers

TIP

● Choose a wet or dull day to visit as there is plenty to see and do to fill a morning or afternoon.

The Museo Nazionale della Scienza e della Tecnologia "Leonardo da Vinci" is one of the world's largest science and technology museums, with around 10,000 scientific exhibits and displays.

Early beginnings The oldest of the three museum buildings (the Monumental Building) is the Olivetan Monastery, built in Renaissance style in the 16th century. Although much has been altered, it still has two beautiful cloisters. The site became a military hospital and barracks under Napoleon. It opened as a museum in 1953 with an exhibition on Leonardo da Vinci, to coincide with the fifth centenary of his birth.

Vast collections The museum has 16 interactive laboratories where visitors can learn about

Clockwise from far left: the cloisters of the early-16th-century Olivetan Monastery—home to the Science Museum; children enjoying themselves in Lab Leonardo; Leonardo da Vinci Parade; steam locomotives in the Railway Pavilion

science and technology, including cutting-edge issues such as biotechnology and robotics; children enjoy the hands-on approach. There are also two separate buildings, devoted to rail, air and sea transport: steam and electric trains are in the reconstructed art nouveau station (the Train Pavilion), while aircraft and ships can be found in the Aero-Maritime Pavilion.

Planning your visit This museum can appear vast and daunting the first time you come so decide what you most want to see before your visit. The Leonardo Gallery is fascinating, though most of the explanations are in Italian only. If you take children, it's best to head for the interactive labs, huge boats, steam trains and aircraft. You can also visit the submarine *Toti* outside the Monumental Building.

THE BASICS

museoscienza.org

✚ E6

✉ Via San Vittore 21, 20123

☎ 02 485 551

🕐 Tue–Fri 10–6, Sat and holidays 10–6.30. Closed 1 Jan, 24 and 25 Dec

🍴 Refreshment area

Ⓜ Sant'Ambrogio

🚌 50, 58, 94

♿ Good

💲 Expensive

❓ Submarine *Toti* tours may be unavailable because of heat or cold

Navigli

TOP 25

Now being spruced up, the Navigli area is central to eating out and nightlife in the city

THE BASICS

⊞ E8–F9

✉ Extends west of Piazza Maggio along Ripa di Porta Ticinese and south along Alzaia Naviglio Pavese

🚇 Porta Genova

🚌 59; tram 2, 3

♿ Good; some steps over bridges

Armani Silos

armani.com/silos

⊞ Off map at F8

✉ Via Bergognone 40, 20144

☎ 02 9163 0010

❓ See website for opening hours, prices and public transport information

Museo delle Culture (Mudec)

mudec.it

⊞ Off map at F8

✉ Via Tortona 56, 20144

☎ 02 54917

❓ See website for opening hours, prices and public transport information

Canal cruises

neiade.com; autostradale.it

HIGHLIGHTS

● Excellent selection of restaurants and bars
● Antiques market on last Sunday of each month
● Boat trips

Named for its navigable canals, until 1979 this area once hummed with barge traffic bringing goods into the city. Now, its buildings are being spruced up and it's evolving into an increasingly vibrant arts and nightlife quarter.

The atmosphere There's been extensive renovation, and it continues, so don't expect picture-postcard canals and quaysides. Enjoy the towpaths and water, the gentrified buildings, the artisan shops and the great bars, restaurants and nightlife of the surrounding streets. It's an area for strolling, or take a canal cruise. Come on the last Sunday of the month, when over 400 antique stalls line the waterside. There are two state-of-the-art attractions, the Armani Silos (▷ 35, panel) and the Museo delle Culture.

Armani Silos Fashion aficionados will love this aggressively contemporary space that's home to a museum entirely dedicated to Giorgio Armani. There are more than 30 pieces to admire, including many from his couture line.

Museo delle Culture Designed by British superstar architect David Chipperfield, this spectacular revamped industrial building houses a permanent collection from Milan's holdings of art and artifacts from all over the world. Its main draw is the series of temporary exhibitions staged throughout the year; past shows have featured artists such as Jean-Michel Basquiat, Gustav Klimt and Frida Kahlo.

View of the church (below); a replica of the Roman statue of Constantine (right)

San Lorenzo Maggiore

This huge fourth-century basilica may have been the chapel of the imperial Roman palace. The greatest treasure is the Sant'Aquilino Chapel, once entirely covered in frescoes and mosaics.

Founded on a Roman temple The church is in the Ticinese quarter, outside the Roman walls, southwest of the city. It is also known as San Lorenzo alle Colonne, after the colonnade outside the church, dating from the second and third centuries. The 16 columns and the section of architrave were probably part of a temple and were placed here in the fourth century when construction began on the basilica. Built with marble from Roman buildings nearby, the basilica was founded on what was thought to be a Roman amphitheater. It was subsequently rebuilt in the 12th century, with further rebuilding between 1573 and 1619 by Martino Bassi.

Beautiful chapel You can't miss the church—it has the largest dome in Milan. The interior, octagonal in form and crowned by the dome, is striking for its sheer size. Inside, make for the Cappella di Sant'Aquilino, which may have been added as a mausoleum; its small chapel houses the saint's remains in a silver urn. The 12th-century fresco of *The Deposition* is at the entrance to the chapel, on the left-hand side. Here you will find the fourth- or fifth-century mosaics of *Christ and the Apostles*, and *Elijah on the Chariot of Fire*. Steps behind the altar take you down to the church's foundations.

THE BASICS

sanlorenzomaggiore.com

🔢 F7

✉ Corso di Porta Ticinese 35, 20123

☎ 02 8940 4129

🕐 Mon–Fri 8.30–12.30, 3–6.30, Sat, Sun 9–1, 3–7

Ⓜ Missori

🚌 94; tram 3, 15

♿ Good

🎫 Free; Cappella di Sant'Aquilino inexpensive

HIGHLIGHTS

● Cappella di Sant'Aquilino
● Fourth/fifth-century mosaics
● 12th-century fresco
● The view of the church from Parco delle Basiliche, the garden behind the church

More to See

BASILICA DI SANT'EUSTORGIO

santeustorgio.it

The unassuming neo-Romanesque facade of the Basilica di Sant'Eustorgio belies the wonderful earlier interior architecture and superb frescoes inside. The original church was founded by St. Eustorgius in the fourth century but was destroyed by Frederick Barbarossa in 1162. Reconstruction began in 1190, lasting several centuries. This included the building of the bell tower in 1306, the first in Milan to be fitted with a clock. The final alteration came in 1865 with the building of the facade seen today. The adjoining monastery is the property of the Diocesan museum and has 17th- and 18th-century religious relics and art from the Basilica.

🛉 F8 🖂 Piazza Sant'Eustorgio 1, 20122 ☎ Church and museum: 02 5810 1583 ⏰ Church: Mon–Sat 7.45–5, Sun 9.30–11, 12.30–5; museum: Tue–Sun 10–6 🚋 Tram 3, 9, 29, 30 ♿ Good (ramp to church) 🎟 Church free; museum moderate

CORSO DI PORTA TICINESE

This street is bisected by one of the remaining medieval gates surrounding the heart of Milan: Porta Ticinese. The area is popular with younger shoppers as its trendy, retro clothing and accessory boutiques are less expensive than the designer shops farther north. Its bohemian atmosphere makes it a fun place to visit and it also has several good traditional *trattorie*.

🛉 F7–F8 🖂 Extends from Largo Carrobbio down to Piazza Sant'Eustorgio 🚋 Tram 3

PARCO DELLE BASILICHE

Named after the basilicas of San Lorenzo and Sant'Eustorgio, this is a pleasant park in the southeast of the city. A pathway flanked by roses links the two basilicas—with the busy Via Molino delle Armi in between. Once one of the least desirable spots in the city, it now fortunately affords a more pleasurable experience.

🛉 F7 🖂 Southeast of city, 20123 ⏰ Dawn–dusk 🚋 94; tram 3

Porta Ticinese—one of the original gateways to the city, leading to Corso di Porta Ticinese

Museums to Canals

Begin at one of the city's finest museums, visit churches along the way, retreat to peaceful gardens and finish up by the canals.

DISTANCE: 3.2km (2 miles) **ALLOW:** 2 hours plus stops

START

MUSEO NAZIONALE DELLA SCIENZA ⊞ E6 ⊜ Sant'Ambrogio

1 If you are keen on science, visit the Museo Nazionale della Scienza (▷ 84–85) in Via San Vittore. Turn right out of the museum and continue along to cross over Via Carducci.

2 Ahead is the lovely Basilica di Sant'Ambrogio (▷ 82–83). Take the path to the left and follow it right the way round the church. Turn right into Piazza Sant'Ambrogio.

3 Ahead is the former monastery, now housing the Catholic university. Leave these buildings on your right and take Via Necchi, the next right.

4 Carry on into Via San Pio V and then turn left into Via Lanzone. At Via Circo look left for the remains of the Circo Romano. Back on Lanzone, bear right into Via Torino.

END

NAVIGLI ⊞ E8 ⊜ Porta Genova 🚌 59; tram 2, 3

8 Turning to the right from the piazza brings you to the Navigli (▷ 86) district, an ideal spot to explore or lunch by the canals.

7 In the park is the Museo Diocesano, with its fine collection of religious art. At the far end of the park is Sant'Eustorgio (▷ 88). Exit here and turn right alongside the church and then left back onto Corso di Porta Ticinese. Carry on down to Piazza XXIV Maggio.

6 Continue to San Lorenzo Maggiore (▷ 87) on your left, and on through the Antica Porta Ticinese, the original entry point into the city. Take the first left for a break in the small park (Basiliche ▷ 88).

5 Cross Largo Carrobbio; take the second right into Corso di Porta Ticinese.

Shopping

BIFFI
biffi.com

The place to shop for classic men's and women's designer names; watch for new emerging talent. Clothes for the sporty, younger customer are across the street.

🔁 F7 ✉ Corso Genova 6, 20123 ☎ 02 8311 6052 🚇 Porta Genova, Sant'Ambrogio

BIVIO
biviomilano.it

Rare in Italy, these two stores, one for men and one for women, sell barely used, but second-hand, high-end fashion and accessories. Everything is bang on trend, in superb condition, and just right for the season.

🔁 F7 ✉ Via Gian Giacomo Mora 4 and 14, 20123 ☎ 02 5810 8691 🚋 94; tram 2, 14

MAURO LEONE
mauroleone.com

Great shoes at great prices are Mauro Leone's hallmark, so come here for a fantastic range of beautifully hand-made-in-Italy shoes, heels, ballerinas and boots. Styles change with the seasons, and they also sell other labels, with prices normally well under €100.

🔁 F8 ✉ Corso di Porta Ticinese 103, 20123 ☎ 02 5810 5041 🚇 Missori 🚋 Tram 2, 3

POURQUOI MOI
In Italy, it's only in Milan that vintage is truly appreciated and this quirky store specializes in outstanding pieces, both clothes and accessories, from the 1960s to the 1980s. The stock changes constantly, but always features top labels—check out their FB page to see what's new.

🔁 F9 ✉ Ripa di Porta Ticinese 27, 20143 ☎ 339 579 2838 🚇 Porta Genova

RAPONI
tessutiraponi.it

Mouthwatering fabrics in silk, crisp linen, cotton and wool, including fine Italian silks in solid, classic and contemporary patterns, plus needlework accessories, ribbons and trimmings. Even if you don't sew, step in to feast your eyes on the large selection available.

🔁 F8 ✉ Via Pietro Panzeri 10, 20123 (corner of Via Panzeri) ☎ 02 8940 4367 🚇 XXIV Maggio 🚋 Tram 9, 29, 30

ROSSANA ORLANDI
rossanaorlandi.com

This quintessential Milanese concept store and gallery occupying an old factory building aims to fill your home with cutting-edge contemporary design. The work of some of Europe's most interesting young designers can be found here, in the shape of furniture and home accessories. There's art on sale too, and a tempting café in a lovely outdoor space, used for events.

🔁 E6 ✉ Via Matteo Bandello 14/16, 20123 ☎ 02 467 4471 🚇 Sant'Ambrogio

MARKETS

Markets fill the waterfronts around the canals, notably Mercato del Sabato on Viale Papiniano (🔁 E7) on Saturday, which offers great designer-label bargains in clothes, shoes and bags, and there is a flea market (Fiera di Senigallia) at Darsena, on Viale d'Annunzio (🔁 F8) also on Saturday. A huge antiques market stretches alongside the canals on the last Sunday of each month. Elsewhere in the city other good general markets are at Via San Marco (🔁 G3) on Monday and Thursday mornings, Via G. Zuretti (🔁 Off map at K1) on Wednesday morning and Via Crema (🔁 K9) on Friday morning.

Entertainment and Nightlife

LE BICICLETTE

lebiciclette.com

Sleek, modern bar and restaurant with changing art exhibitions in an area increasingly popular for nightlife. Happy hour and buffet from 6 until 9.30.

🔲 F7 ✉ Via G. B. Torti 2, 20123 ☎ 02 5810 4325 🚇 Sant'Ambrogio

CUORE

cuoremilano.it

This nifty little bar and venue, tucked away down a side street, is lively, friendly and welcoming—expect good drinks, funky decor and crowds who flock here for rock and roll, jazz, DJs and live music.

🔲 F7 ✉ Via Gian Giacomo Mora 3, 20123 ☎ 02 5811 8311 🚇 Sant'Ambrogio

MAG CAFÉ

magcafemilano.myadj.it

You'll find this intimate bar right on the waterfront; inside, it's cosy indeed, with deep chairs, rugs and clever lighting adding to the charm. The drinks here are imaginative, using herbs and house-blended syrups to create some great flavors.

🔲 E8 ✉ Ripa di Porta Ticinese 43, 20143 ☎ 02 3956 2875 🚇 Porta Genova

OLD FOX PUB

oldfoxpub.it

Keeping the original fittings of the former local milk bar, this is the quintessential British pub. Good selection of beers and the owners have a penchant for whiskies. Lots of English pub grub, Italian sports on screen and accompanying music. Occasional theme music nights (check details first). Buffet and happy hour are good value from 6 to 9.

🔲 E7 ✉ Piazza Sant'Agostino, 20123 ☎ 02 8940 2622 🚇 Sant'Agostino

TEATRO ARSENALE

teatroarsenale.it

The place to come for searing comedy, cutting-edge dramas and groundbreaking acting. Tickets are available from the venue itself, and can be bought online. Most performances are in Italian only.

🔲 F7 ✉ Via Cesare Correnti 11, 20123 ☎ Box office 02 8321 1999, information 02 832 1999 🚇 Sant'Ambrogio

LE TROTTOIR

letrottoir.it

Not just a bar, Le Trottoir is a platform for creative new talent. Events from live rock bands and jazz artists to poetry readings, plus inexpensive cocktails.

🔲 F8 ✉ Piazza XXIV Maggio 1, 20122 ☎ 02 837 8166 🕐 Daily 11am–late 🚋 Tram 2, 3

VOLT

voltclub.it

Serious clubbers will love the music and vibe of this club, with its fabulous sound and light systems, chic all-black decor and impressive DJ line-up. Check the website for different genres.

🔲 G7 ✉ Via Molino della Armi 16, 20123 ☎ 342 797 6858 🚇 Missori 🚋 Tram 3

MILANESE BARS

Most Milanese bars are open all day until 2 or 3am. They serve a vast selection of beers, wines, aperitifs, cocktails and non-alcoholic drinks, and most have a selection of snacks—some double as cafés. Many of Milan's bars have introduced an early-evening happy hour when drinks are cheaper. If you sit down for waiter service you will pay a premium, whether inside or out. The procedure when standing up is to pay for what you want at the cash desk, then take your receipt to the bar and repeat your order.

Where to Eat

PRICES

Prices are approximate, based on a 3-course meal for one person.

€€€ over €55
€€   €25–€55
€   under €25

AL PONT DE FERR (€€–€€€)

pontdeferr.it

Traditional *osteria* with brick archways and wood paneling. Chef Ivan Milani does an excellent set menu, both seasonal and regional, using fine, locally sourced produce.

➕ E8 ✉ Ripa di Porta Ticinese 55, 20143
☎ 02 8940 6277 🕐 Tue–Sun lunch, dinner
🚇 Porta Genova

AMICI DEL LIBERTY (€€)

amicidelliberty.com

This traditionally decorated restaurant is open until 2am. The accent is on fish. They cater to vegetarians and vegans.

➕ D7 ✉ Via Savona 20, 21044 ☎ 02 839
4302 🕐 Mon–Fri lunch, dinner; Sat dinner.
Closed Aug 🚇 Sant'Agostino

CANTINA DELLA VETRA (€€)

cantinadellavetra.it

Venerable, real Italian restaurant, close to the Porta Ticinese. Lasagne, stew, hearty pastas and grilled meats.

➕ G7 ✉ Via Pio IV 3, 20122 ☎ 02 8940
3843 🕐 Mon–Sat lunch, dinner, Sun brunch
12 and 2, dinner 🚇 Missori

IL GIARDINETTO (€€)

osteriailgiardinetto.it

Warm *osteria* resplendent with plants. Excellent and regional cuisine based on Milanese and Piacentina tradition.

➕ E8 ✉ Via Tortona 17, 21044 ☎ 02 839
3807 🕐 Mon–Fri lunch, dinner; Sat dinner
🚇 Sant'Agostino

KAZAN (€–€€)

kazansushi.it

Good when you fancy a change from Italian food. Choose from an extensive menu that includes sushi, Japanese noodle and meat dishes and Chinese specialties. Daily lunch and dinner specials are good value.

➕ F7 ✉ Corso di Porta Ticinese 70, 21044
☎ 02 8366 0979 🕐 Daily 11–3, 6–midnight
🚇 Missori 🚋 Tram 2, 3

OSTERIA DEL BINARI (€€)

osteriadelbinari.com

In summer eat outside in the garden. Lombardy and Piedmont cooking is the specialty. Friendly service.

➕ E8 ✉ Via Tortona 1/3, 20144 ☎ 02
2839 5095 🕐 Mon–Sat dinner only 🚇 Porta
Genova

RISTORANTE SANT'EUSTORGIO (€€)

Nice venue overlooking the square and the church, just off Porta Ticinese. Stop here for a pizza or traditional dish. Good homemade food using local produce.

➕ F8 ✉ Piazza Sant'Eustorgio 6, 20122
☎ 02 5810 1396 🕐 Daily 12–11.30
🚇 Missori 🚋 Tram 2, 3

TRATTORIA OR OSTERIA?

In general, a trattoria is an unpretentious, family-run concern, often with a regular clientele of local people who drop in when they do not want to cook themselves. The *osteria* used to be the most basic eating place of all, where simple dishes were washed down with jugs of local wine. Nowadays, however, the word has been adopted by some of the most expensive or touristy establishments. Don't judge by the name alone: generally the smarter the premises, the pricier the restaurant.

Farther Affield

Outside the city center, options include taking in one of Milan's most stimulating museums, visiting splendid churches, paying homage to its iconic football teams, or heading out of Milan for a water-park or a trip to magical Lake Como.

Top 25

HangarBicocca

TOP 25

● *The Seven Heavenly Palaces* by Anselm Kiefer
● *La Sequenza*, outside the entrance, by Fausto Melotti
● The Cubo buildings

TIPS

● It will take you around 30 minutes travel time by metro, longer by bus.
● It's a 10-minute walk from the metro to the Hangar.
● There are excellent kids' workshops and guided tours catering for 4- to 14-year-olds.

An abandoned industrial site and its buildings have been converted into one of Europe's most innovative, huge and exciting spaces for contemporary art, hosting temporary exhibitions and a permanent installation.

The project In 2004 the Pirelli company took the decision to convert a former aircraft hangar on a disused factory site into an exhibition space. Its mission would be to produce, promote and exhibit contemporary art, and to help the general public connect with the art world.

The buildings The complex has three buildings: the entrance Shed; the Cubo, once a locomotive manufacturing workshop, now the main exhibition space; and the Navate a 30m

Clockwise from left: The Seven Heavenly *Palaces by Anselm Kiefer; interior exhibition space; oustide the HangarBicocca*

(98ft) high building that houses a permanent sculptural installation. Together, they cover 15,000sq m (161,460sq ft), making the Hangar one of the largest art spaces in Europe.

The art Temporary exhibitions usually run for six months. The main draw for many visitors though is the permanent sculptural installation *The Seven Heavenly Palaces* (2004–15) by Anselm Kiefer, commissioned for the opening of the Hangar. It consists of seemingly precarious stacked towers of concrete and lead, with a challenging theme of individuality and spirituality. Just take in these huge structures and come away with your own impressions. They are surrounded by five large-scale paintings installed in 2015, whose subjects reflect the same themes as the towers and form part of the installation.

THE BASICS

hangarbicocca.org

✚ See map ▷ 95

✉ Via Chiese 2, 20126

☎ 02 6611 1573

🕐 Thu–Sun 10–10

🍴 Iuta Bistrot on site

🚉 Sesto Mirelli, Ponale

🚌 51, 87, 728

♿ Excellent

🎟 Free

❓ Lectures, film shows, guided tours, workshops and concerts: check website for details

More to See

ACQUATICA

acquaticapark.it

A great family day out, especially in the summer heat, this water park has pools, thrilling slides, fountains, tubes, river rides, twisting water chutes and artificial beaches.

See map ▷ 94 ✉ Via G. Airaghi 61, 20153 ☎ 02 4820 0134 ⏲ Jun–Sep daily 10–7 🚇 San Siro then bus 423, San Siro then bus 80, De Angeli then bus 80, Bisceglie then bus 76 💷 Expensive

CIMITERO MONUMENTALE

The neo-Romanesque cemetery (1866) covers an area of 250,000sq m (2,700,000sq ft) in the northwest of the city. Eminent Milanese and other Italians, including novelist Manzoni and the poet Salvatore Quasimodo, are buried in the Famedio (House of Fame). Fine sculpture.

F1 ✉ Piazzale Cimitero Monumentale, north end of Via Manzoni, 20154 ☎ 02 8846 5600 ⏲ Tue–Sun 8–6 🚇 Monumentale, Garibaldi 🚊 2, 4, 10, 14, 33 ♿ Good 💷 Free

IDROSCALO

idroscalo.info

This huge artificial lake was once a seaplane landing site; it's now a year-round recreational center whose attractions include a water park, swimming pool, children's playground and more. Check the website for the event program.

See map ▷ 95 ✉ Via Circonvallazione 29, 20090, near Linate ☎ 02 7020 8197 ⏲ Apr–Oct daily 8am–9pm, Nov–Mar 8–5 🚇 Aeroporto Linate then bus 73, 183 💷 Expensive

LEONARDO'S HORSE

The largest bronze equine statue in the world at 7m (23ft) high, this is a replica of a monument that Leonardo da Vinci was commissioned to build in 1482. It didn't get beyond model stage and was finally cast in 1999 in the US. It rather appropriately stands outside the horse-racing stadium, the Ippodromo (▷ 104) in San Siro.

See map ▷ 94 ✉ Piazzale dello Sport, San Siro 20151 🚇 Lotto 🚊 Tram 16

The majestic Leonardo's horse

MUSEO DEL GIOCATTOLO E DEL BAMBINO

museodelgiocattolo.it

A huge toy museum 3km (2 miles) east of the city. Displays include 18th-century toys, tin sci-fi toys and papier-maché dolls. Exhibits have themes such as Pinocchio, the Golden Age of the Toy (1880–1915), Theater and Circus.

➕ See map ▷ 95 ✉ Via Gianni Rodari 3, 20134 ☎ 340 150 9192 🕐 Check website or call 🚇 Lambrate, then bus 729 ♿ Good 💵 Moderate

MUSEO INTER & AC MILAN

sansirotour.com

This museum is in the San Siro stadium, where both of Milan's soccer teams play. There are more than 3,000 items on display, including trophies, flags and memorabilia relating to Milan's two teams, Inter and AC. There are guided tours of the stadium daily except Sunday and when matches are in progress.

➕ See map ▷ 94 ✉ Stadio Giuseppe Meazza (San Siro), Gate 21, Via Piccolomini 5, 20151 ☎ 02 404 2432 🕐 Daily 9.30–6 (last entry 5); the museum is closed during sporting events 🚇 San Siro Stadio: Lotto, then shuttle bus on match days; bus 49; tram 16 ♿ Good 💵 Expensive

PARCO LAMBRO

This large park to the east of the city is a good place to relax and escape the heat in high summer. It was designed to mirror the natural Lombardy countryside with the River Lambro meandering through the middle and has numerous lakes and ponds. Team sports and rowing are popular activities here.

➕ See map ▷ 95 🚇 Udine 🚌 55

STA MARIA ALLA FONTANA

This serene 16th-century church, with its beautiful cloister, was once thought to be by Leonardo da Vinci. In fact it's the work of Amedeo, constructed by Milan's French governor, Charles d'Amboise, on the site of a holy spring, to which he attributed his cure from illness.

➕ See map ▷ 95 ✉ Piazza Santa Maria alla Fontana 11, 20159 ☎ 02 688 7059 🕐 Daily 8–12, 3–7 🚇 Garibaldi, Zara 🚌 6, 90, 91; tram 4 ♿ Good 💵 Free

STA MARIA DELLA PASSIONE

Milan's second-largest church, dating from the 14th and 15th centuries, has a Greek cross plan, extended by a nave and side chapels. It's famous for its mainly 16th- and 17th-century paintings and frescoes by leading Lombard artists. Don't miss *The Fasting of St. Charles* by Daniele Crespi, perhaps Milan's finest 17th-century work.

➕ K5 ✉ Via Conservatorio 14, 20122 ☎ 02 7602 1370 🕐 Mon–Sat 8–12, 3.30–5, Sun 9.30–12, 3.30–6.30 🚇 San Babila 🚌 54, 61 ♿ Good, one step 💵 Free

STAZIONE CENTRALE

milanocentrale.it

Majestic Stazione Centrale is not just Milan's main railway station but is the biggest in all Italy. Although it was not completed until 1931, it was designed in 1912 and its style is more characteristic of art nouveau than the heavy Fascist architecture of the 1930s.

➕ K1 ✉ Piazzale Duca d'Aosta, 20124 ☎ 89 20 21 🕐 24 hours, tourist information Mon–Sat 8–7, Sun 9–12.30, 1.30–6 🚇 Centrale 🚌 42, 60, 82, 92; tram 2, 5, 33 ♿ Good

Excursions

THE BASICS

Distance: 48km
(30 miles)
Journey time: 1 hour
🚆 Regular service from
Garibaldi FS
🔆 Via Gombito 13
☎ 035 242 226
visitbergamo.net

BERGAMO

Northeast of Milan in the southern foothills of
the Alps, Bergamo could not be more different
from Italy's business capital.

Remarkably unspoiled, historic Bergamo
crowns a steep hill. The city is divided into
the medieval Città Alta (Upper Town), within
16th-century walls, and the contrasting
modern, traffic-filled Città Bassa (Lower Town).
A funicular transports you to Città Alta and its
picturesque cobbled alleyways and medieval
and Renaissance buildings. Visit Piazza del
Duomo, where the Duomo pales against the
Renaissance porch of the Basilica of Santa
Maria Maggiore and lavish facade of the
Cappella Colleoni, built as a mauseoleum for
Bergamo's most famous mercenary. There are
superb views from the Torre del Gambito (263
steps). The highlight of the lower town is the
Galleria Accademia Carrara and its collection of
Venetian, Bergamesque and other works of art.

THE BASICS

Distance: 93km
(58 miles)
Journey time: 2 hours
🚆 Regular service from
Stazione Centrale
🔆 Piazza del Comune 5
☎ 0372 23233;
turismocremona.it

CREMONA

A quiet market town on the banks of the River
Po, Cremona has been the heart of the violin-
making industry since 1566.

The greatest violin maker, Antonio Stradivari,
was born here in 1644, and is commemorated
in the Museo del Violino, a state-of-the-art
museum that contains the city's historic collection of violins, and the tools used to make
them. You can watch a luthier (violin-maker)
working, and don't miss the wooden room
where videos of the violins in action are pro-
jected. In the middle of town is Piazza del
Comune, a fine medieval square with beautiful
medieval monuments: the highest bell tower in
Italy, the Romanesque/Gothic cathedral, the
octagonal Baptistry (1167) and the Palazzo del
Comune (1206–45).

LAKE COMO

Leave the buzz of Milan and within an hour or so you can be at Lake Como, one of the loveliest of the northern Italian lakes.

Surrounded by high mountains and rugged green hills, Como is smaller than Lake Maggiore and Lake Garda, but it has the longest perimeter (170km/106 miles), and is Italy's deepest lake, plunging to 372m (1,220ft) between Argegno and Nesso.

Its beautiful shoreline, wonderful views, year-round agreeable climate and plethora of pretty villages, small towns, lavish villas and gardens add to its charms, while the opportunities for walking, boat trips and villa visits make this a must-see destination.

The picturesque *centro storico* (historic center) of the town of Como is still partly enclosed by 12th-century walls. It's a lovely place to wander, taking in the architecture and pretty squares, notably the piazzas of Cavour, Alessandro Volta and San Fedele. You'll see many tempting silk shops; Como's wealth was built on the industry and it's still Europe's most important producer—you can learn more in the Museo della Seta (silk museum).

The main sights to visit are the Basilica di San Fedele (Piazza San Fedele; open 8–12, 3.30–7), whose interior, with its three naves and apses is decorated with 16th- and 17th-century frescoes, illuminated by light from a beautiful rose window. Como's marble-clad Duomo (cathedral) is worth a look too; mainly Gothic in style, it dates from the 14th to 18th centuries.

It's a short cable-car ride (funicolarecomo.it) from Piazza Alcide de Gasperi in Como up the hill to Brunate, a quiet little village with spectacular views of the surrounding mountains and lake, and plenty of walking opportunities in the vicinity.

THE BASICS

Distance: 50km
(31 miles)

Journey time: 30 min to 1 hour depending on departure station

🚆 Regular service from Stazione Centrale to Como town (30 min); Cadorna (1 hour)

ℹ️ Stazione San Giovanni, Como ☎ 342 007 6403; Via Albertolli, Como
☎ 31 349 3068
lakecomo.com

Museo della Seta
museosetacomo.com
✉ Via Castelnuovo 9
☎ Tue–Fri 10–6, Sat 10–1
♿ Good
💵 Expensive

Duomo
✉ Piazza del Duomo
☎ Mon–Sat 10.30–5, Sun 1–4.30

THE BASICS

illagomaggiore.com
Distance: 85km
(53 miles)
Journey time: Stresa
(70 min)
🚆 Regular services from
Milano Centrale and
Milano Porta Garibaldi
ℹ️ Stresa: Piazza Marconi
16 ☎ 0323 30150.
Stresa
Ferries: half-hourly to
the Borromean Islands
from Stresa. Day ticket:
expensive
ℹ️ Cable-car: stresa-
mottarone.it; journey time
20 min
💶 Expensive

LAKE MAGGIORE

Italy's second largest lake, Maggiore is ringed with green hillsides, beyond which rise the Swiss Alps. Its shores are strung with beguiling towns, the slopes behind strewn with villas and gardens, while on the lake itself lie the star attractions, the Borromean Islands.

For a taste, head for the lakeside Stresa, where you can explore the old center's cobbled streets, or stroll along the lakeside promenade. Ferries leave from Piazza Guglielmo Marconi to the islands of Bella, Madre and Pescatori. Isola Bella is famous for Palazzo Borromeo and its terraced gardens, Madre has a botanical garden filled with exotic and rare subtropical plants, and Pescatori retains the atmosphere of the fishing village it once was. You could also take the 20-minute cable-car trip up to Monte Mottarone (1,492m/4,895ft) for glorious views of the lake and surrounding mountains.

THE BASICS

Distance: 39km
(24 miles)
Journey time: 45 min
🚆 Service from Stazione
Centrale to either Pavia
(for the town) or Certosa
di Pavia
ℹ️ Via del Comune 18,
corner of Piazza della
Vittoria; visitpavia.com
Certosa di Pavia
prolococertosadipavia.it
☎ 352 925613
🕐 Tue–Sun 9–11, 2.30–5

PAVIA

Pavia is graced by fine Romanesque and medieval buildings, but what really draws the crowds is the nearby 14th-century monastery.

Certosa di Pavia (8km/5 miles north of Pavia) is one of the most extravagant religious complexes in northern Italy—the exuberant facade in multitoned marble has a wealth of inlay and sculpture. During its century-long construction tastes changed, and what you see today is an architectural complex that traces the transformation from Gothic via Renaissances to mannerist style. Join a tour to see the best parts of the monastery. Pavia's rich heritage of art and architecture is reflected in its Renaissance cathedral, whose architects include Leonardo da Vinci, Bramante and Amadeo, several fine medieval churches and the Visconti castle.

Entertainment and Nightlife

AC MILAN AND INTER

acmilan.com; inter.it

Catch one of Italy's top soccer clubs, AC Milan or Inter, at the San Siro on alternate weekends during the season. Tickets for matches sell out fast, so it is best to buy in advance on the website or, for Inter, from branches of Banca Popolare di Milano, for AC, from branches of Cariplo bank.

🔲 Off map at A2 ✉ Via dei Piccolomini 5, 20151 🕐 Sep–Jun 🚇 Lotto then free bus before matches 🚊 Tram 16

ALCATRAZ

alcatrazmilano.it

Rock-oriented live music and disco venue frequented by the occasional famous face.

🔲 Off map at G1 ✉ Via Valtellina 25, 20121 ☎ 02 6901 6352 🚇 Maciachini 🚊 90, 91, 92; tram 3, 4

AUDITORIUM DI MILANO

laverdi.org

This superb, modern, 140-seater multi-purpose hall is home to the Orchestra Sinfonica di Milano Giuseppe Verdi, noted for its innovative musical programming. The venue puts on symphony concerts, choral works and chamber music; it's also noted for its jazz and light music.

🔲 Off map at F9 ✉ Largo G. Mahler, 20136 ☎ 02 8338 9401/2/3 🚇 Romolo, then trolley bus 90, 91 🚊 59, 71

BLUE NOTE

bluenotemilano.com

Perfect venue for listening to top-quality international jazz. Also a restaurant and a bar. You get the chance to catch some big international names.

🔲 Off map at G1 ✉ Via P. Borsieri 37, 20159 ☎ 02 690 1688 🚇 Garibaldi

CENTRO SPORTIVO MARIO SAINI

milanosport.it

This tennis facility has an open-air clay court and 12 indoor synthetic courts. Equipment is available to rent. Non-members welcome, but tennis whites are appreciated. The center also has a gym and a 50m swimming pool.

🔲 Off map at M4 ✉ Via A. Corelli 136, 20134 ☎ 02 756 2741 🕐 Mon–Sat dawn–dusk 🚊 38

DUCALE MULTISALA

cinenauta.it

The Ducale has been converted from an old cinema into a modern four-screen movie house with a pleasant bar.

🔲 B8 ✉ Piazza Napoli 27, 20146 ☎ 199 208 002 🚇 Porta Genova

GOLF CLUB MILANO

golfclubmilano.it

This prestigious 18-hole golf course 30 minutes from Milan is close to the town of Monza. Pro shop, driving range, pool and restaurant.

🔲 Off map to north ✉ Viale Mulini San Giorgio 7, 20052 Monza ☎ 039 303 081

MEAZZA STADIUM

Renamed after Giuseppe Meazza, one of Italy's all-time great soccer players, in 1980, this famous stadium is more commonly called San Siro, after the district surrounding it. A remarkable design, the building gives the impression that it is wrapped up by the spiraling access flights. It was originally built in 1926 as a gift from Piero Pirelli, the then-president of AC Milan, and could only seat 10,000. A second tier was added in 1955 and a third plus a fiber-glass roof supported by 12 cylindrical concrete towers was added in 1987, making the stadium's capacity over 85,000.

IPPODROMO DEL GALOPPO/TROTTING

ippodromisnai.it

For horseracing fans there is a full calendar of flat racing events from March to November. In the separate arena across the road, trotting races take place throughout the year, except for the month of August.

⊞ Off map at A2 ✉ Piazzale dello Sport, San Siro 20151 ☎ 02 482 161 Ⓜ Lotto 🚊 Tram 16

MAGAZZINI GENERALI

magazzinigenerali.it

Spread over two floors, this buzzing nightclub offers a great range of evening events to choose from. Check out the regular dance evenings on the dance floor, or head there for one of the guest DJ appearances, live performances or party nights.

⊞ Off map at J9 ✉ Via Pietrasanta 14, 20141 ☎ 02 539 3948 Ⓜ Lodi Ⓜ 90; tram 24

PLINIUS

multisalaplinius.com

Built in the 1930s and now housing six screens, this multistory multiplex cinema, occupying a former theater, shows mainstream blockbusters and Italian art-house films, and streams opera and ballet from across the world.

⊞ M2 ✉ Viale Abruzzi 28–30, 20131 Ⓜ Loreto, Lima

POGUE MAHONE

poguemahones.pub

If you require a night away from the typical Italian bar—to drink Guinness and watch soccer, for example—head for this popular Irish pub. Live bands are often featured.

⊞ K8 ✉ Via V. Salmini 1, 20135 ☎ 199 20 80 02 Ⓜ Porta Romana

LE ROVEDINE

rovedine.com

Milan's only public golf course lies 6km (4 miles) outside the city. There are two parkland courses, beautifully landscaped with mature trees, set around a lake. You can go putting, practice your driving, play 9 or 18 holes, hire clubs and a cart or go swimming in the outdoor pool.

⊞ Off map to east ✉ Via Karl Marx 18, Noverasco di Opera, 20090 ☎ 02 5760 6420

TEATRO CARCANO

teatrocarcano.com

First opened to the public in 1803, the theater underwent major changes in the 1980s. Theatrical productions include staged versions of films, and it is also used for lectures by the university.

⊞ J7 ✉ Corso di Porta Romana 63, 20122 ☎ 02 5518 1362/5518 1377 Ⓜ Crocetta

TUNNEL CLUB

tunnel-milano.it

An unusual space created in a converted warehouse under the central station. A variety of live music, DJ evenings, poetry readings, film shows and exhibitions, and you can enjoy cocktails at the bar. Prices are lower than other more conventional venues in the city.

⊞ K1 ✉ Via Sammartini 30, 20125 ☎ 339 403 2702 Ⓜ Centrale FS

ITALIAN GRAND PRIX

The Italian Grand Prix at Monza ranks alongside Monte Carlo as one of the glitziest Grands Prix on the Formula 1 circuit. Plenty of stars and models watch the race under a sea of red Ferrari flags. Ticket information can be found on the website.

⊞ Off map to north ✉ Parco di Monza, 20052 Monza ☎ 039 248 2212; monzanet.it 🕐 Sep 🚉 From Stazione Centrale

Where to Eat

<table>
<tr><td colspan="2">PRICES</td></tr>
<tr><td colspan="2">Prices are approximate, based on a 3-course meal for one person.</td></tr>
<tr><td>€€€</td><td>over €55</td></tr>
<tr><td>€€</td><td>€25–€55</td></tr>
<tr><td>€</td><td>under €25</td></tr>
</table>

AIMO E NADIA (€€€)

aimoenadia.com

Today, chefs Alessandro Negrini and Fabio Pisani remain true to the values of this excellent restaurant, founded more than 60 years ago by Aimo and Nadia. Using the finest and freshest produce, they produce stunningly imaginative modern Italian food.

🔲 Off map A7 ✉ Via R. Montecuccoli 6, 20146 ☎ 02 416 886 🕐 Mon–Fri lunch, dinner; Sat dinner only 🚇 Primaticcio

BE BOP (€€)

beboptristorante.it

Elegant pizza and pasta restaurant, where cooking is also directed at vegetarians and coeliacs—90 percent of the menu is gluten free.

🔲 G8 ✉ Viale Col di Lana 4, 20136 ☎ 02 837 6972 🕐 Lunch, dinner 🚇 Porta Genova 🚊 Tram 3

BERBERÉ (€–€€)

berberepizza.it

This upscale pizzeria offers a choice of dough—classic, sourdough or yeast-free. Alongside the classic toppings, you'll find superb combinations such as pumpkin, wild mushrooms and taleggio cheese or *cavolo nero* (black cabbage) with sharp provolone cheese, mustard and leeks. Desserts are excellent, with delicate sorbets and a rich chocolate trio.

🔲 Off map ✉ Via Sebenico 21, 20124 ☎ 02 3670 7820 🕐 Daily dinner, Sat–Sun lunch 🚇 Isola

LA BOTTEGA DEL GELATO (€)

labottegadelgelato.it

This *gelateria*, not far from the central station, sells delicious ice cream, including peach, passion fruit, melon and tamarillo.

🔲 L2 ✉ Via Pergolesi 3, 20124 ☎ 02 2940 0076 🕐 Thu–Tue 🚇 Caiazzo

LA COZZERIA (€)

lacozzeria.it

Each dish here is based upon a kilogram (about 2lb) of mussels. Chefs curry them, pepper them, make them into a soup or serve them with cream, spices or liqueurs.

🔲 L8 ✉ Via L. Muratori 6, 20135 ☎ 02 5410 7164 🕐 Tue–Sun lunch, dinner 🚇 Porta Romana

DA GASPARE (€€)

ristorantedagaspare.com

Despite refreshingly low prices, Da Gaspare stands head and shoulders above the rest of Milan's fish restaurants. Lobster, mussels, crab and more crustaceans. Tasty desserts, too. Small, uncomfortable and often noisy, but the regulars keep flooding back.

🔲 B5 ✉ Via Carlo Ravizza 19 20149 ☎ 02 4800 6409 🕐 Thu–Tue lunch, dinner 🚇 Buonarroti

ERBA BRUSCA (€€–€€€)

erbabrusca.it

This distinctly chic but low-key restaurant is located on the outer reaches of the city. It is surrounded by a vegetable garden, where much of the produce comes from. It offers original and innovative food with influences from the Middle East. The menu is short and changes daily, but might include risotto with black garlic, chick pea gnocchi or rabbit stuffed with figs.

Off map ✉ Alzaia Naviglio Pavese 296, 20142 ☎ 02 8738 0711 🕐 Wed–Sun lunch, dinner 🚇 Abbiategrasso

LATTERIA MAFFUCCI (€€–€€€)

Well and truly off the beaten path, this tiny restaurant has no written menu, the food depending totally on the day's best and freshest produce, which is explained to you. The emphasis is on fish. Dinner consists of a tasting menu of eight little starters, followed by a choice of two *primi* and *secondi* (first and main courses), dessert and coffee.
Off map ✉ Via Privata Angiolo Maffucci, 20158 ☎ 02 375 614 🕐 Tue–Sun 8.30am–11.30pm 🚇 Maciachini

MANGIAR1 DI STRADA (€–€€)

mangiaridistrada.com
The name means street food, generally offal and entrails. All are served slow-cooked with piquant sauces and gravies. If that seems a bit too much, the menu also offers mainstream Italian favorites.
Off map ✉ Via Lorenteggio 269, 20152 ☎ 02 415 0556 🕐 Daily lunch, dinner 🚇 Lorenteggio

RATANÀ (€€–€€€)

ratana.it
The menu here changes seasonally, and combines Milanese classics such as saffron-infused risotto and deep-flavored *ossobucco* (shin of veal) with more modern interpetations of old favorites.
Off map ✉ Via Gaetana de Castillia 28, 20124 ☎ 02 8712 8855 🕐 Daily lunch, dinner 🚇 Isola

IL SOLITO POSTO (€€)

ilsolitoposto.net
Since 1888 this trattoria has been serving customers in the heart of Como, a few steps from the lake shore. Dishes

are lovingly prepared and delicious. The *carpaccio* is superb and the restaurant is known for its *osso buco*.
Off map ✉ Via Lambertenghi 9, 22100 Como ☎ 031 271 352 🕐 Daily 12–3, 7–11.15 🚈 From Milano Centrale

TRATTORIA TRE TORRI (€€)

The trip to Bergamo would be worth it just to dine in this trattoria in the heart of the walled medieval fortress. In the summer, savor beautifully prepared local cuisine in the garden.
Off map ✉ Piazza Mercato del Fieno 7/A, 24129 Bergamo ☎ 035 244 474 🕐 Daily lunch and dinner 🚈 From Milano Centrale, then funicular to old town

IL VICOLETTO (€€)

ristorantevicoletto.com
Light, delicious food, firmly rooted in tradition, are the keynotes of this popular restaurant, loved by locals. The menu changes regularly with the seasons, but is always excellent and the chef prides himself, rightly, on the presentation.
Off map ✉ Vicolo del Pocivo 3, Stresa ☎ 0323 932102 🕐 Fri–Wed lunch, dinner 🚈 Train from Milano Centrale or Porta Garibaldi

---

IL CONTO

The bill (check), *il conto*, usually includes extras such as *servizio* (service). Iniquitous cover charges (*pane e coperto*) have now been outlawed, but some restaurants still try to get round the regulations. Only pay for bread (*pane*) if you have asked for it. Proper receipts—not a scrawled piece of paper—must be given by law. If you receive a scrap of paper, which is more likely in a pizzeria, and have doubts about the total, ask for a proper receipt (*una fattura* or *una ricevuta*).

There is a wide range of accommodations in Milan. You can choose from world-class deluxe hotels in historic buildings, chic boutique hotels or family-run smaller hotels that haven't changed much in 30 years.

Introduction

You'll find the full range of hotel options in Milan as you would in any prosperous city. Prices can be steep, as establishments in the upper price range outnumber inexpensive options.

Best to Book

Although Milan has plenty of accommodations, the city is a major commercial hub with a constant flow of businesspeople, so you will need to book in advance—especially if there is a trade fair or fashion show taking place at the same time. As there tend to be more commercial visitors than tourists, Milan's hotels are usually more in demand during the week, leaving more rooms available on weekends, when hotels may drop their prices. As a large proportion of the hotels are located in clusters on the perimeter areas around the city, it can be difficult to secure a place to stay right in the *centro* without paying high prices.

Saving Money

Nowadays, you'll probably reserve online, so remember room rates fluctuate daily depending on demand, and it may be worth keeping your nerve and holding out for a far cheaper last-minute booking. Alternatively, call for a little gentle bargaining, particularly at quieter times. Some hotels will put another bed in a room for an extra 35 percent, ideal for families. Rates vary according to season, sometimes as much as 25 percent, and increase dramatically when there are trade events taking place.

TIPS

● If you haven't booked in advance, the local visitor information office will have lists and may be willing to make reservations for you.
● It's perfectly acceptable to ask to see the room before you decide to stay somewhere.
● You will have to show your passport at check-in, as hotels are required to collect guest details.
● Check-out time is normally 11am–12, but hotels will usually store your luggage till the end of the day.

Budget Hotels

PRICES

Expect to pay under €160 per night for a double room in a budget hotel.

43 STATION HOTEL

43stationhotel.com

Ideally situated for city-break travelers, this modern, comfortable, quiet hotel lies very near the central station. The decor is stylish and relaxing. Extras include superfast WiFi, hyper-allergenic-bath products and superior matresses.

➕ J1 ✉ Via Fabio Filzi 43, 20124 ☎ 02 2217 9900 Ⓜ Duca d'Aosta

HOTEL ARISTON

aristonhotel.com

This is an excellent value, modern hotel within walking distance of the Duomo. Rooms and bathrooms are not huge, but the public rooms are spacious and a good breakfast comes with the room.

➕ F7 ✉ Largo del Carrobio 2, 20123 ☎ 02 7200 0556 Ⓜ Missori

HOTEL DUE GIARDINI

hotelduegiardini.it

Excellent value hotel near Stazione Centrale. No elevator but staff are on hand to help with luggage. All rooms have modern comforts and private bathrooms. Breakfast is served in the garden when weather permits.

➕ K2 ✉ Via Benedetto Marcello 47, 20124 ☎ 02 2952 1093 Ⓜ Centrale FS

HOTEL NUOVO

hotelnuovomilan.com

Good value for a central spot. All 36 rooms are clean and compact—most have telephone, TV and, some, a private bathroom. Can be noisy at night.

➕ H6 ✉ Piazza Cesare Beccaria 6, 20122 ☎ 02 8646 4444 Ⓜ San Babila

HOTEL SEMPIONE

hotelsempionemilan.com

Near the station and a couple of stops into Milan's heart, this hotel is a good find. Expect well-equipped, if smallish, functional rooms, a good breakfast and value weekend-break offers. WiFi in public areas only.

➕ J3 ✉ Via C. Finocchiaro Aprile 11, 20124 ☎ 02 657 0323 Ⓜ Repubblica

LONDON HOTEL

hotellondonmilano.com

You get a warm welcome at this central hotel, where the comfy lounge is a popular place to gather. Overlooking a tranquil back street, the 30 large rooms are spartan and slightly dated.

➕ G5 ✉ Via Rovello 3, 20121 ☎ 02 7202 0166 Ⓜ Cairoli

SAN FRANCISCO

hotel-sanfrancisco.it

Close to the Giardini Indro Montanelli, this well-renovated hotel offers modern rooms and a warm welcome. The excellent breakfast buffet, proximity to public transport and good mid-range shopping, and the bonus of its own garden, make this a good choice.

➕ Off map at M1 ✉ Viale R. Lombardia 55, 20131 ☎ 02 236 0302 Ⓜ Piola

SHOWER OR BATH?

Most hotel rooms in Milan have a private bathroom—unless your hotel is exceptionally basic—which will normally contain a sink, flush toilet, bidet and bath or shower. In much of Italy, showers are far more common than baths, owing to the scarcity and expense of water. You will notice a cord in the bathroom: this is a legal requirement for emergencies and summons help when pulled.

Mid-Range Hotels

ANTICA LOCANDA LEONARDO

anticalocandaleonardo.com

The rooms have been renovated, and are tastefully furnished, from an authentic antique style to a more classic style, while the walls are adorned with works of art by contemporary artists.

✚ E5 ✉ Corso Magenta 78, 20123 ☎ 02 4801 4197 Ⓜ Cadorna

ANTICA LOCANDA SOLFERINO

anticalocandasolferino.it

Tucked away in a quiet cobbled street, this delightful old-fashioned *pensione* is very friendly. The simple but spacious rooms, decorated with antiques, have pretty balconies. There are only 11 rooms, so book in advance.

✚ H3 ✉ Via Castelfidardo 2, 20121 ☎ 02 657 0129 Ⓜ Moscova

BAVIERA

hotelbaviera.com

This primarily business hotel ticks boxes for tourists too. The public areas and many of the rooms have been renovated, breakfasts are good, there's a nice bar, and you can easily walk from the hotel to the main city-center sights and districts. Book online for the best deals.

✚ K3 ✉ Via P. Castaldi 7, 20124 ☎ 02 659 0551 Ⓜ Repubblica

BRISTOL

hotelbristolmil.it

Exit the Milano Centrale station via the stairs and you'll find yourself at the front door of this classic hotel. A refined Anglo-French style blends with modern amenities, which include 68 sound-proofed rooms and in-room Jacuzzis and Internet facilities. Helpful English-speaking staff.

✚ K1 ✉ Via D. Scarlatti 32, 20124 ☎ 02 669 4141 Ⓜ Repubblica

CANADA

canadahotel.it

What this glass structure lacks in character it makes up for with 35 pristine, modern rooms that will meet all your needs. There are good views of the Duomo from the eighth floor. About a 10-minute walk from the *centro storico*.

✚ H7 ✉ Via Santa Sofia 16, 20122 ☎ 02 5830 4844 Ⓜ Crocetta

CARLYLE BRERA

hotelcarlyle.com

This sleek modern hotel lies in the Brera, an easy stroll from many of central Milan's main sights. Used by business people, the hotel has comfortable, unfussy rooms, many with baths rather than showers; all have AC and WiFi. Excellent breakfasts are served either inside or out on the enclosed terrace area.

✚ G3 ✉ Corso Garibaldi 84, 20121 ☎ 02 2900 3888 Ⓜ Moscova

CAVOUR

hotelcavour.it

Serious shoppers will find themselves very close to the Quadrilatero d'Oro at this well-run hotel. Rooms are mainly a good size, there's a gym and Turkish bath, excellent public areas and bar and a classy restaurant.

⊞ H4 ✉ Via Fatebenefratelli 21, 20121 ☎ 02 620 001 🚇 Turati

GRAN DUCA DI YORK

ducadiyork.com

Housed in a grand 18th-century building, close to Piazza del Duomo and the Pinacoteca Ambrosiana, this hotel oozes style. Rooms are well-equipped and comfortable, though some are on the small side. It's worth upgrading to a superior room with its own leafy terrace.

⊞ G6 ✉ Via Moneta 1, 20123 ☎ 02 874 863 🚇 Cordusio

HOTEL MICHELANGELO

michelangelohotelmilan.com

Streamlined public areas and more than adequate rooms and bathrooms are the hallmark of this primarily business hotel, easily reached from the airports and the Stazione Centrale. Excellent breakfasts.

⊞ K1 ✉ Piazza Luigi di Savoia 6, 20124 ☎ 02 67551 🚇 Centrale FS

MANIN

hotelmanin.it

A sophisticated, modern hotel on the edge of the prestigious shopping streets. The huge conservatory-garden area is ideal for lunch or a cocktail. Nicely decorated throughout, with 118 spacious bedrooms; some with terrace or balcony overlooking the gardens.

⊞ J3 ✉ Via D. Manin 7, 20121 ☎ 02 659 6511 🚇 Turati

MANZONI

hotelmanzoni.com

There's a quiet and traditional elegance to this comfortable hotel, tucked away on a side street, yet right in the heart of Milan's prestigious shopping area. There's a good range of room sizes; all have high-speed WiFi. The hotel has its own distinctly smart restaurant.

⊞ H5 ✉ Via Santo Spirito 20, 20121 ☎ 02 7600 5700 🚇 Montenapoleone

REGINA

hotelregina.it

A charming 18th-century mansion adorned with antique furniture and paintings. The 43 comfortable rooms have an old-fashioned appeal, with parquet floors and large rugs. It's located close to the Navigli canals. Pretty garden.

⊞ F7 ✉ Via Cesare Correnti 13, 20123 ☎ 02 5810 6913 🚇 Missori

SPADARI AL DUOMO

spadarihotel.com

A small hotel with contemporary art and sculpture displayed against vivid blue decoration. The 39 spacious bedrooms have designer furniture. No restaurant, but snacks are served. A few steps from Teatro alla Scala and Galleria Vittorio Emanuele II.

⊞ G6 ✉ Via Spadari 11, 20123 ☎ 02 7200 2371 🚇 Duomo

UNA MAISON MILANO

gruppouna.it

A few minutes' walk from the Duomo, this boutique-style hotel, with its soothing decor in gray and muted blues and excellent service, provides a calm oasis in hectic Milan.

⊞ G6 ✉ Via G. Mazzini 4, 20123 ☎ 02 726 891 🚇 Duomo

Luxury Hotels

BULGARI MILAN

grandluxuryhotels.com/milan

For the ultimate decadent treat, book into Milan's most stylish and expensive, hotel. Set in a beautiful garden in the Brera, its delights include tranquil rooms with superb bathrooms, a pool, hammam and spa and excellent restaurant. The hotel is famous for its 7–9 *aperitivo*, served daily in the garden.

➕ H5 ✉ Via Privata Fratelli Gabba 7, 20121 ☎ 02 858 051 🚇 Montenapoleone

FOUR SEASONS

fourseasons.com/milan

A beautifully restored 15th-century monastery in the Quad d'Oro set around a cloistered courtyard. The huge opulent reception has frescoes, columns and vaulted ceilings; rooms and suites have restrained elegance and superb comfort.

➕ H5 ✉ Via Gesù 6/8, 21021 ☎ 02 77088 🚇 Montenapoleone

GRAND HOTEL ET DE MILAN

grandhoteletdemilan.it

Since its opening in 1863, the Grand has been welcoming VIPs and celebrities. The hotel provides luxury on a grand scale, from its super-comfortable rooms, its splendid public areas, bars and restaurants, to the up-to-the-minute fitness area and business facilities.

➕ H4 ✉ Via A. Manzoni 29, 20121 ☎ 02 723 141 🚇 Montenapoleone

THE GRAY

sinahotels.com

Facing the renowned Galleria, this stylish hotel is minimalist design at its best: dim lighting and metallic decoration with a splash of red. Framed prints and modern lights enhance the 21 rooms, all with the latest mod cons including hydro tubs.

➕ H5 ✉ Via San Raffaele 6, 20121 ☎ 02 720 8951 🚇 Duomo

PRINCIPE DI SAVOIA

dorchestercollection.com

Meticulous gardens leading up to a majestic white facade give an indication of the sumptuous interior you are about to enter. With a 1930s feel, the rooms of this landmark hotel are adorned with antiques, marble and luxury carpets. The rooms and suites are a generous size. Facilities include indoor pool and fitness and beauty complex.

➕ J3 ✉ Piazza della Repubblica 17, 20124 ☎ 02 62301 🚇 Repubblica

SHERATON DIANA MAJESTIC

marriott.com

Set in pretty gardens, close to Milan's main shopping area, this art deco hotel is the place to be seen; it is popular during fashion shows with models and journalists. The circular foyer has leather chairs and period furniture, and the 107 Imperial-style rooms have elegant marble bathrooms.

➕ K4 ✉ Viale Piave 42, 20129 ☎ 02 20581 🚇 Porta Venezia

STRAF

straf.it

Unconventional modern comfort in a prime spot next to the Duomo. An ultrasleek minimalist look has been created using materials such as raw concrete, iron, slate, burnished brass, gauze-effect glass and scratched mirrors.

➕ H5 ✉ Via San Raffaele 3, 20121 ☎ 02 805 081 🚇 Duomo

Use this section to help you plan your visit to Milan. You will find information about getting around once you are there, as well as useful tips and a language section.

Planning Ahead

When to Go

Milan is primarily a business destination, with little seasonal variation in the number of visitors or cost of hotels, but avoid visiting during major events, such as fashion shows. April, May, June and September are good months to visit. June begins to get hot and it cools off at the end of September with increasing bouts of rain.

TIME

Italy is one hour ahead of GMT, six hours ahead of New York and nine hours ahead of Los Angeles.

AVERAGE DAILY MAXIMUM TEMPERATURES

JAN	FEB	MAR	APR	MAY	JUN	JUL	AUG	SEP	OCT	NOV	DEC
43°F	46°F	54°F	59°F	68°F	73°F	79°F	79°F	70°F	61°F	54°F	45°F
6°C	8°C	12°C	15°C	20°C	23°C	26°C	26°C	21°C	16°C	12°C	7°C

Spring (March to May) is very pleasant, although rain can persist into May.

Summer (June to August) high temperatures bring a humid haze and normally some thunderstorms, which help to clear the air.

Autumn (September to November) gradually turns from showers to heavy rain, and November is dank and wet.

Winter (December to February) Alpine winds make it very cold and there can be heavy frosts and thick fog. December can produce pleasant bright, crisp days.

WHAT'S ON

January *Corteo dei Re Magi* (6 Jan): A Nativity-theme procession travels from the Duomo to Sant'Eustorgio.

February *Carnevale Ambrosiano*: The carnival culminates with a parade on the first Saturday of Lent.

March *MODIT-Milanovendemodo* (early Mar): International fashion show.

Milano–San Remo (third Sat): Milan hosts the start of this famous international bicycle race.

April *Fiera dei Fiori* (Mon after Easter): Fair devoted to flower growing, near Sant' Angelo Franciscan convent.

Stramilano (early Apr): Annual marathon race with over 50,000 competitors.

June *Festa del Naviglio* (first Sun): Festival held along the Navigli canals; concerts, street performers, sports, handicrafts and regional cooking.

July/August *Festival Latino-Americano*: Festival of Latin-American music, handicrafts and cuisine.

September *Gran Premio di Monza*: Formula One Grand Prix of Italy.

October *MODIT-Milanovendemoda* (early Oct): second major fashion show.

December *Festa di Sant'Ambrogio* (4–7 Dec): Festival celebrating Sant'Ambrogio, Milan's fourth-century patron saint and the city's first mayor. Stalls are set up around the Sforza Castle exterior walls and most people take the day off work to attend the market. Also called *Oh Bej! Oh Bej!* after the children's cries of delight in the 16th century.

Milan Online

turismo.milano.it
Milan's main tourist website includes practical information on city sights, restaurants, nightlife, shopping, transport and practical information.

wheremilan.com
Lively and frequently updated site covering every aspect of visiting Milan; particularly good for museum, events and shopping suggestions.

hellomilano.it
English site that is easy to understand and has good up-to-date details on what's on, news, restaurants, nightlife, shopping and general information.

enit.it
The main Italian Tourist Board website carries a wealth of information about the whole country—available in several languages.

emmeti.it
An Italy-based site, in English and Italian, with a good range of information on Milan and links to other sites. It's strong on local events and offers an online hotel-booking service.

initaly.com
An enthusiastic site run by passionate lovers of Italy from the US. It's packed with information and articles about the country, with quirky tips and insider stories, and makes excellent browsing when you're planning your trip.

ciaomilano.it
Easy-to-navigate site in English covering every aspect of Milan; strong on what's on, shopping and nightlife.

lakecomo.is; visitbergamo.net; turismocremona.it; illagomaggiore.it
Official websites for Lake Como, Bergamo, Cremona and Lake Maggiore; all available in English.

TRAVEL SITES

fodors.com
A complete travel-planning site. You can research prices and weather; book air tickets, cars and rooms; pose questions to (and get answers from) fellow travelers; and find links to other sites.

atm.it
Milan's city transport system runs this informative site, where you'll find everything you could possibly want to know, including how to buy the best ticket for your needs—Italian and English.

fsitaliane.it
The official site of the Italian State Railways, with excellent train information.

INTERNET ACCESS

Accessing the internet on your mobile phone can be expensive, depending on where you are from and your service provider.Most hotels offer WiFi access, usually free, though sometimes only in the lobby area. The city launched Open WiFi in 2012, offering free public WiFi in many central piazzas and streets, and in some museums, libraries and civic offices. Go to openwifimilano.it to register.

NEED TO KNOW PLANNING AHEAD

Getting There

For the latest passport and visa information, look up the British embassy website at gov.uk, the United States embassy at it.usembassy. gov, or for Canadians, travel.gc.ca.

INSURANCE

Check the cover provided by your insurance policy and buy any necessary supplements. EU nationals receive reduced-cost emergency medical treatment with the relevant documentation (EHIC for British residents), but travel insurance is still advised.

CUSTOMS REGULATIONS

EU nationals do not have to declare goods imported for their personal use.
The limits for non-EU visitors are 200 cigarettes or 100 small cigars or 250g of tobacco; 1 liter of alcohol (over 22 percent alcohol) or 2 liters of fortified wine; 50g of perfume.

AIRPORTS

There are direct flights from all over the world into Malpensa airport, Milan's main international gateway, while Linate airport, classed as a city airport, handles just Italian domestic and European flights. Visitors from Europe can also arrive by rail or by bus.

52km (32 miles)

Malpensa

Milan ● Linate

FROM MALPENSA

Most flights arrive at Malpensa (tel 02 232323; milanomalpensa-airport.com, 50km (31 miles) northwest of the city. The Malpensa Express train (tel 02 72 494949; malpensaexpress.it) runs to Cadorna–Ferrovie Nord (every 30 minutes, 6.53am–9.53pm; €13, journey time 40 minutes). Stamp your ticket in the machine on the platform before boarding. The Malpensa Shuttle (tel 02 5858 3185; malpensashuttle. com) leaves from outside the terminal to Stazione Centrale (every 30 minutes, 6.35am–11.35pm; €12, journey time 50–60 minutes). Other bus operators from terminals 1 and 2 are: Terravision (terravision.eu) and Autostradale (autostradale.it). Both leave every 20 minutes (journey time 50 minutes); buy tickets (€8) in the terminal or on board. Taxis to the city can take up to 75 minutes depending on the traffic and are expensive (€75–€100). Make sure you get an official white taxi. If someone approaches you offering a taxi, this will cost you more. Taxis returning to Malpensa should display a sticker *"taxi autorizzato per il servizio aeroportuale lombardo"* on the screen.

FROM LINATE

Linate, the closest airport, is only 6km (4 miles) east of the city (tel 02 232323; milanolinate-airport.com). The most convenient option for getting into the city is by taxi; official white cabs line up outside the terminal (€40, but check the cost before). ATM city bus No. 73 (every 20 minutes, 6.35am–1.05am; journey time 25 minutes) goes to Piazza San Babila (tickets €2 from vending machines). STARFLY coach service run a service to Stazione Centrale (every 30 minutes, 5.40am– 9.35pm; €5; journey time 25 minutes).

ARRIVING BY BUS

The majority of domestic and international buses arrive at the main terminus in Piazza Castello. Autostrade Viaggi (autostradaleviaggi. com) is the major bus company connecting Milan with the rest of Italy.

ARRIVING BY CAR

It is not advisable to drive into Central Milan. The city is divided into segments with a one-way system and you can only enter the city at a limited number of points. The "Sosta Milano" parking system is extremely difficult to under-stand and unless you have parking at your hotel it is really better not to use a car. If you do bring a car be aware that fuel stations in the city close for lunch, on Saturday afternoons and all day Sunday. Do not leave your car on yellow lines or in areas marked by a tow-away symbol. The bottom line is you are far better off using the excellent public transport system.

ARRIVING BY RAIL

Most international and domestic trains arrive at Stazione Centrale, in the northeast of the city, although the Malpensa Express arrives at Cardona–Ferrovie Nord, closer to the city center. There are easy connections to the rest of the city from here: The station is on Metro lines 2 and 3, taxis line up outside the entrance, and several trams and buses stop right outside.

HANDY HINT

In the land of the Vespa, it's tempting to hire a scooter (*motorino*) and Milan has many scooter rental outlets. But scooters are not for the fainthearted, and if you've never ridden one in a big city, Milan is not the place to start.

CONSULATES

- **British Consulate**
  ✉ Via San Paulo 7
  ☎ 02 723 001
  🕐 Mon–Fri 9.30–12.30, 2–4
- **US Consulate**
  ✉ Via Principe Amedeo 2/10 ☎ 02 290 351
  🕐 Mon–Fri 8.30–5.30
- **Canadian Consulate**
  ✉ Piazza Cavour 3
  ☎ 02 6269 4238
  🕐 Mon–Fri 9–1; email before visiting: consul. canada.milan@gmail.com

Getting Around

VISITORS WITH DISABILITIES

Milan is rapidly upgrading its facilities for visitors with disabilities. Many hotels and restaurants are accessible and the situation is improving in museums and monuments. A growing number of buses have ramps or lower floors for wheelchair users and some underground trains are wheelchair-friendly: look for the logo on the side of the train. The AIAS organization in Milan, provides details of access for specific hotels, restaurants and the main tourist sights, and public transport. Their website is in English.
AIAS Milano
milanopertutti.it
✉ Via Paolo Montegazza, 20156

Milan has an efficient integrated transportation system comprising trams, buses and a Metro, which is easy to use (atm.it).

BUSES AND TRAMS
Bus and tram routes cover the whole city and also follow the Metro routes overground. Both are very efficient and run about every 10 minutes. They do get crowded, especially during rush hour—take care of your belongings. Bus and tram stops have a yellow sign displaying the route and a timetable. All buses and trams in Milan are orange except for the tourist trams, which are one of the best ways of seeing the city.

THE METRO
The Metro is the easiest and fastest option, though you may have to combine it with a bus or tram. The Metro consists of four lines: red MM1, green MM2, yellow MM3 and blue *passante ferroviario* (suburban loop). These intersect at the hub stations of Stazione Centrale, Duomo, Cardorna and Loreto.

TICKETS
Tickets must be purchased in advance and stamped in a machine once on board. Fines are handed out to anyone caught without a ticket. A single (€1.50) is valid for 90 minutes from validation and can be used on the entire system for as many bus and tram trips as you want, plus one Metro journey (a carnet of 10 tickets is available at €13.80). One- and two-day travel cards (€4.50/€8.25) are also available. These last 24/48 hours respectively from time of first stamping; once stamped you do not need to do it again. Tickets are sold at tobacconists, bars, newsstands, tourist offices and Metro stations. The network runs 6am–midnight, with night buses continuing until 1.30am.

TAXIS
Official taxis in Milan are normally white and the charges are reasonable. It is almost impossible

to hail a passing cab so it's best to call (Radiotaxi tel 02 4040; 02 8585; 02 6969) when you want one—they usually arrive quite quickly—or go to a taxi rank (stand) at Piazza del Duomo, Stazione Centrale, Piazza della Scala, Piazza San Babila, Piazza A. Diaz and Via Manzoni.

SCOOTERS, MOPEDS AND BICYCLES
Even experienced riders or cyclists should be careful if using this mode of transport on Milan's congested roads. There are several places in the city that hire these forms of transport: try Biancoblu (Via Gallarate 33, tel 02 3082 2430; biancoblu.com) for scooters and mopeds; AWS (Via Ponte Seveso 33, tel 02 6707 2145) for bicycles.

WALKING
Walking is the best way to get around, but beware of busy traffic when crossing the road.

ORGANIZED SIGHTSEEING
A bus tour, run by Autostradale (tel 02 3391 0749), leaves Piazza del Duomo (Tue–Sun 9.30am) for a three-hour tour to most of Milan's main sights, accompanied by a multi-lingual commentary; cost €65 and includes entry to *The Last Supper*, the Duomo and La Scala. For a fascinating overview of the city take the City Sightseeing Milano bus (tel 02 867 131; city-sightseeing.it)—two different hop-on hop-off guided tours with multilingual recorded commentary. It departs from Piazza Castello (daily all year; tours leave 9.30–5.45; 6.30 in summer) and lasts for about 1 hour 30 min-utes; cost €25; reduced cost for children (5–15 years) €10. You can buy tickets for both tours at the tourist information offices.

An alternative is to view the city on foot. Walking Tours of Milan (Via G. Marconi 1, tel 02 7252 4301) run a tour every Monday from the APT tourist office. A Friend in Milan (tel 02 2952 0570; friendinmilan.co.uk) provides guided walking tours throughout the city.

STUDENT VISITORS
● Bring an ISIC card to get reductions on museum fees.
● If you intend to stay at youth hostels, you need to get a youth hostel card before leaving for Italy.

TOURIST OFFICES
Principal tourist office: Galleria Vittorio Emanuele II, corner of Piazza della Scala ☎ 02 8845 5555 🕔 Mon–Fri 9–7, Sat 9–6, Sun 10–6
Stazione Centrale ☎ 02 7252 4360 🕔 Daily 8am–9pm

Essential Facts

MONEY

The euro (€) is the official currency of Italy. Banknotes are in denominations of 5, 10, 20, 50, 100, 200 and 500 euros, and coins in denominations of 1, 2, 5, 10, 20, 50 cents and 1 and 2 euros. Credit cards are widely accepted and most banks have ATMs.

WOMEN VISITORS

● Women are generally safe visiting Milan alone.
● After dark avoid Parco Sempione, the rail station and poorly lit streets away from the middle of the city.

ELECTRICITY

● Voltage is 220 volts and sockets take two round pins.

LOST PROPERTY

● Council lost property office: Via Friuli 30, tel 02 8845 3900, open Mon–Fri 8.30–4.
● Central railway left luggage office: Stazione Centrale (1st floor of Galleria Partenze), tel 02 6371 2667, open daily 6am–1am.
● It is imperative to report losses of passports to the police (▷ Emergency Numbers panel, opposite).

MAIL

● Get general post office information on 803 160 or at poste.it.
● Main post office: Via Cordusio 4 tel 02 7248 2508, open Mon–Fri 8–7, Sat 8.30–12.
● There is another big post office at the Stazione Centrale: Piazza Duca d'Aosta, tel 02 6707 2150, open Mon–Fri 8–7, Sat 8.30–9.
● You can buy stamps (francobolli) from post offices or from tobacconists displaying a white T sign on a dark background.
● Post boxes are small, red and marked Poste or Lettere. The slot on the left is for addresses within the city and the slot on the right is for other destinations.

MEDICINES AND MEDICAL TREATMENT

● In a medical emergency, call 118 or go to the Pronto Soccorso (casualty department or emergency room) of the nearest hospital.
● Poison Antidote Center: tel 02 6610 1029.
● Pharmacies are indicated by a large green or red cross.
● A free emergency number gives details of your nearest pharmacy (tel 02 85781). The Central Station pharmacy is open 24 hours a day, in the first-floor departures gallery.
● There are several night pharmacies, including those located in: Piazza del Duomo 21 (tel 02 861161); Via Boccaccio 26 (tel 02 469 5281); Corso Magenta 96 (tel 02 4800 6772).

OPENING TIMES
● Banks: Mon–Fri 8.30–1.30, 3–4.
● Post offices: Mon–Fri 8.30–1.50, Sat 8–12. The main city post offices stay open at lunchtime and close at 7.
● Shops: normally 9.30–1, 3.30–7.30.
● Museums: see individual entries.
Main tourist attractions often stay open longer. No two are the same.

PUBLIC HOLIDAYS
1 Jan: New Year's Day; 6 Jan: Epiphany; Easter Sunday; Easter Monday; 25 Apr: Liberation Day; 1 May: Labor Day; 2 Jun: Republic Day; 15 Aug: Assumption; 1 Nov: All Saints' Day; 8 Dec: Immaculate Conception; 25 Dec: Christmas Day; 26 Dec: St. Stephen's Day. Most places of interest close on New Year's Day, 1 May and Christmas, while others close on all public holidays.

TELEPHONES
● There are few telephone centers in the city: Via Santa Rita di Cascia 68 (open daily 24 hours); Piazza Caiazzo (open daily 24 hours).
● Phone cards (*carta, scheda or tessera telefonica*) are the most practical way to use a public phone as few public telephones take coins.
● Directory enquiries: tel 12.
● International directories: tel 176.
● International operator: tel 170.
● Cheap rate is all day Sunday and 9pm–8am (national) on other days; 10pm–8am (international).
● To call Italy from the UK, dial 00 followed by 39 (the code for Italy) then the number. To call the UK from Italy dial 00 44 then drop the first zero from the area code.
● To call Italy from the US dial 011 followed by 39. To call the US from Italy dial 00 1.
● Milan's area code (02) must be dialed even if you are calling from within the city.
● GSM and Tri-band phones can be used with an Italian SIM card.

EMERGENCY NUMBERS
● Police ☎ 113
● Police (Carabinieri) ☎ 112
● Police headquarters (for foreigners and passport office) ✉ Via Montebello 26 ☎ 02 62261
● Fire ☎ 115
● Ambulance ☎ 118
● Breakdown service Automobile Club di Milano (ACI) ☎ 803 116

NEWSPAPERS
The daily city newspaper, *Il Corriere*, includes listings for plays, music and cinema. Other Italian dailies, *La Repubblica* and *Corriere della Sera*, produce weekly supplements with up-to-date listings of cultural events in the city. The tourist office has a free newspaper, *Hello Milano*, and online service (hello milano.it) in English, giving information and listings on the arts, plays, nightlife and a little on shopping. Foreign newspapers can usually be bought after about 2.30 on the day of issue from booths (*edicole*) in the city. European editions of the *Financial Times*, *USA Today* and *International Herald Tribune* are also available.

Language

All Italian words are pronounced as written, with each vowel and consonant sounded. The letter *h* is a silent modifier; *c* is hard, as in "cat", except when followed by *e* or *i*, when it becomes the soft *ch* of "cello". The letter *g* is soft (as in "giant") when followed by *i* or *e*—*giardino, gelati;* otherwise hard (as in "gas")—*gatto*. Words ending in *o* are almost always masculine (plural: -*i*); those ending in *a* are generally feminine (plural: -*e*). Use the polite third person (*Lei*) to strangers and the informal second person (*tu*) to friends.

USEFUL WORDS	
yes	*sì*
no	*no*
please	*per favore*
thank you	*grazie*
you're welcome	*prego*
excuse me!	*scusi*
where	*dove*
here	*qui*
there	*là*
when	*quando*
now	*adesso*
later	*più tardi*
why	*perchè*
who	*chi*
may I/can I	*posso*
good morning	*buon giorno*
good afternoon/ good evening	*buona sera/ buona notte*
hello/good-bye (informal)	*ciao*
hello (on the telephone)	*pronto*
I'm sorry	*mi dispiace*
left/right	*sinistra/destra*
open/closed	*aperto/chiuso*
good/bad	*buono/cattivo*
big/small	*grande/piccolo*
with/without	*con/senza*
more/less	*più/meno*
hot/cold	*caldo/freddo*
early/late	*presto/ritardo*
now/later	*adesso/più tardi*
today/tomorrow	*oggi/domani*
when?/do you have?	*quando?/avete?*

NUMBERS	
1	*uno, una*
2	*due*
3	*tre*
4	*quattro*
5	*cinque*
6	*sei*
7	*sette*
8	*otto*
9	*nove*
10	*dieci*
20	*venti*
30	*trenta*
40	*quaranta*
50	*cinquanta*
100	*cento*
1,000	*mille*

EMERGENCIES

help!	*aiuto!*
stop, thief!	*al ladro!*
can you help me, please?	*può aiutarmi, per favore?*
call the police/an ambulance	*chiami la polizia/ un'ambulanza*
I have lost my wallet/ passport	*ho perso il mio passaporto/ il mio portafoglio*
where is the police station?	*dov'è il commissariato?*
where is the hospital?	*dov'è l'ospedale?*
I don't feel well	*non mi sento bene*
first aid	*pronto soccorso*

COLORS

black	*nero*
brown	*marrone*
pink	*rosa*
red	*rosso*
orange	*arancia*
yellow	*giallo*
green	*verde*
light blue	*celeste*
sky blue	*azzuro*
purple	*viola*
white	*bianco*
gray	*grigio*

USEFUL PHRASES

how are you? (informal)	*come sta/stai?*
I'm fine	*sto bene*
I do not understand	*non ho capito*
how much is it?	*quant'è?*
do you have a room?	*avete camere libere?*
how much per night?	*quanto costa una notte?*
with bath/shower	*con bagno/doccia*
when is breakfast served?	*a che ora è servita la colazione?*
where is the train/ bus station?	*dov'è la stazione ferroviaria degli autobus?*
where are we?	*dove siamo?*
do I have to get off here?	*devo scendere qui?*
I'm looking for ...	*cerco...*
where can I buy ...?	*dove posso comprare...?*
a table for ... please	*un tavolo per... per favore*
can I have the bill?	*il conto*
we didn't have this	*non abbiamo avuto questo*
where are the toilets?	*dove sono i gabinetti?*

DAYS/MONTHS

Monday	*lunedì*
Tuesday	*martedì*
Wednesday	*mercoledì*
Thursday	*giovedì*
Friday	*venerdì*
Saturday	*sabato*
Sunday	*domenica*
January	*gennaio*
February	*febbraio*
March	*marzo*
April	*aprile*
May	*maggio*
June	*giugno*
July	*luglio*
August	*agosto*
September	*settembre*
October	*ottobre*
November	*novembre*
December	*dicembre*

Timeline

NAPOLEON'S RULE

The city of Milan welcomed the arrival of Napoleon, and indeed it was he who brought forward the idea of the unification of Italy. His contributions to the city included reforming the educational and legal system, inaugurating the building of new public offices and establishing new museums and art galleries. He even saw the completion of the Duomo so he could hold his coronation there as the self-appointed "king of Italy". However, after 18 years of rule and high taxation the Milanese people were relieved when Napoleon was defeated at the Battle of Waterloo and Milan was returned to Habsburg rule.

222BC The Romans defeat the Gauls. Milan becomes the most important city in the Western Roman Empire after Rome.

AD374 Sant'Ambrogio (St. Ambrose) becomes Bishop of Milan. The city flourishes.

452 The city is devastated by Attila the Hun, then again in 489 by the Goths.

568 Lombards invade and take power.

774 Rebirth of the city under the rule of Charlemagne.

1042 Milan becomes an autonomous city.

1162 German Emperor Frederick I invades. Milan is burned to the ground.

1176 Battle of Legnano gives independence to northern Italian cities.

1277 Rise of the Visconti family. The Duomo is commissioned in 1386.

1450 Rise of the Sforza family; for 50 years art and commerce flourish.

1499 Louis XII of France occupies Milan.

1540–1706 Milan under Spanish rule.

1706 Control of the city passes to the Austrian Habsburgs.

From left to right: Milan's awesome cathedral; detail of a statue at the Castello Sforzesco; relaxing in the grounds of the castle; gloriously illuminated—the Duomo at night

1796–1814 Napoleonic rule. New building work is undertaken.

1804 Napoleon's coronation at the Duomo.

1815 Napoleon is defeated and Milan is handed back to the Habsburgs.

1848 Unification—Milan becomes part of Italy. The population increases to 240,000.

1919 Fascist movement founded by Benito Mussolini in Milan.

1939–1945 Milan suffers serious bomb damage during World War II.

1950s Milan leads Italy's economic recovery.

1960s Industrial and student unrest. Acts of terrorism take place.

1984 Lega Lombarda formed; separatist party which becomes Lega Nord in 1991.

1994–2006 Milanese Berlusconi's right-wing party holds national power; era marked by economic stagnation, corruption and scandal.

2017 Work on life science research institute, the Human Technopole, Europe's largest scientific and socio-economic program, started.

2018 Plans announced to ban cars from the city center when air quality is poor.

EARLY DAYS

During the Bronze Age, the Ligurians were the first to settle in the Po Valley, and by the sixth century BC the powerful Etruscans were well ensconced. By 338–386BC, after various skirmishes, the area was ruled by the Gauls.

SANT'AMBROGIO

The patron saint of Milan, whose feast day is on 7 December, was Bishop of Milan from AD374–397. As a result of his integrity and skill in negotiating between the Catholic and Arian church officials, Milan became an important religious hub.

Index

Milan 25 Best

WRITTEN BY Jackie Staddon and Hilary Weston
UPDATED BY Sally Roy
SERIES EDITOR Clare Ashton
COVER DESIGN Jessica Gonzalez
DESIGN WORK Liz Baldin
COLOR REPROGRAPHICS Ian Little

© AA Media Limited 2020 (registered office: Fanum House, Basing View, Basingstoke, Hampshire RG21 4EA, registered number 06112600).

Published in the United Kingdom by AA Publishing.

ISBN 978-1-6409-7204-9

FIFTH EDITION

Printed and bound in China by 1010 Printing Group Limited

10 9 8 7 6 5 4 3 2 1

A05671
Maps in this title produced from mapping © MAIRDUMONT / Falk Verlag 2018 and data available from openstreetmap.org © under the Open Database License found at opendatacommons.org
Transport map © Communicarta Ltd, UK

We would like to thank the following photographers, companies and picture libraries for their assistance in the preparation of this book.

2/18t AA/M Jourdan; 4tl AA/C Sawyer; 5 Koba Samurkasov/Alamy Stock Photo; 6cl AA/M Jourdan; 6c AA/C Sawyer; 6cr AA/M Jourdan; 6bl AA/M Jourdan; 6bcl AA/M Jourdan; 6bcr Photodisc; 6br Photodisc; 7cl Fototeca; 7c AA/M Jourdan; 7cr AA/C Sawyer; 7bl AA/J Tims; 7bc AA/P Bennett; 7br Brand X Pics; 10tr AA/M Jourdan; 10tcr AA/M Jourdan; 10cr AA/M Jourdan; 10/11br AA/M Jourdan; 11tl AA/M Jourdan; 11tcl AA/M Jourdan; 11cl AA/C Sawyer; 13tl Archivio Fotografico I.A.T. Ufficio Informazioni e Accoglienza Turistica della Provincia di Milano palcoreale.; 13cl Brand X Pics; 13bcl Digitalvision; 13bl Brand X Pics; 14tcr AA/M Jourdan; 14cr AA/M Jourdan; 14br AA/S McBride; 14tr AA/M Jourdan; 16tr AA/M Jourdan; 16cr AA/M Jourdan; 16br AA/C Sawyer; 17tl AA/C Sawyer; 17cl AA/J Holmes; 17bl AA/J Holmes; 18tr AA/M Jourdan; 18tcr Museo Nazionale della Scienza e della Tecnologia; 18cr AA/M Jourdan; 18br Brand X Pics; 19(iv) Museo Nazionale della Scienza e della Tecnologia; 20 AA/M Jourdan; 24/5 Alinari Archives; 26tl AA/M Jourdan; 26tr AA/M Jourdan; 27tl AA/M Jourdan; 27tr AA/M Jourdan; 28l © Walter Carrera, Poldo Pezzoli Museum, Milan; 28r The Bridgeman Art Library; 29l AA/M Jourdan; 29r Alinari Archives; 30tl Stefano Politi Markovina/Alamy Stock Photo; 30cl Peter Forsberg/Alamy Stock Photo; 30/1 Peter Forsberg/Shopping/Alamy Stock Photo; 32-33t AA/M Jourdan; 32b AA/M Jourdan; 33b Seat Archive/Alinari Archives; 34t AA/M Jourdan; 35t AA/M Jourdan; 36t AA/M Jourdan; 37t AA/M Jourdan; 38t Digitalvision; 39t AA/C Sawyer; 40 AA/T Harris; 41 AA/M Jourdan; 44l AA; 44/5t AA/C Sawyer; 44/45b AA/M Jourdan; 45r Ethan Rambacher/Alamy Stock Photo; 46 Riccardo Sala/Alamy Stock Photo; 47 Elio Villa/Alamy Stock Photo; 48 AA/M Jourdan; 48tr AA/M Jourdan; 49cr Carol Barrington/Alamy Stock Photo; 50l Valentino Visentini/Alamy; 50r HermesMereghetti/Alamy; 51 Adam Eastland/Alamy Stock Photo; 52l ASK Images/Alamy Stock Photo; 52r Bailey-Cooper Photography/Alamy Stock Photo; 53tr www.vittorebuzzi.it/Alamy; 53tl AA/C Sawyer; 54-55t AA/M Jourdan; 54b AA/M Jourdan; 55br www.sanfedeleartefede.it; 56t AA/M Jourdan; 57t AA/C Sawyer; 58t AA/M Chaplow; 58c Photodisc; 59t AA/E Meacher; 60t David Wasserman/brandxpictures; 61 AA/P Bennett; 64 © CuboImages srl/Alamy; 65tl AA/M Jourdan; 65c Saporetti photo credits; 65tr AA/M Jourdan; 66l Alain Machet (3)/Alamy; 66tr AA/M Jourdan; 67 AA/M Jourdan; 68 AA/M Jourdan; 69l AA/M Jourdan; 69r AA/M Jourdan; 70 © World Pictures/Alamy; 71t Seat Archive/Alinari Archives; 72tl Alinari Archives; 72/73 AA/M Jourdan; 74t AA/M Jourdan; 74b AA/M Jourdan; 75t AA/M Jourdan; 76t Photodisc; 77t Brand X Pics; 78t AA/A Kouprianoff; 79 AA/M Jourdan; 82/83 Seat Archive/Alinari Archives; 84l Museo Nazionale della Scienza e della Tecnologia; 85tl Museo Nazionale della Scienza e della Tecnologia; 85tr Museo Nazionale della Scienza e della Tecnologia; 85c Museo Nazionale della Scienza e della Tecnologia; 86 Fabrizio Robba/Alamy Stock Photo; 87tl AA/M Jourdan; 87tr AA/M Jourdan; 88t AA/M Jourdan; 88b Archivio Fotografico I.A.T. Ufficio Informazioni e Accoglienza Turistica della Provincia di Milano; 89t AA/M Jourdan; 90t AA/M Jourdan; 91t Digitalvision; 92t AA/T Souter; 93 AA/P Bennett; 96/7 Courtesy Pirelli Hangar Bicocca. Photo Agostino Oslo; 97t Lorenzo Palmeri. Courtesy Pirelli Hangar Bicocca; 97c Courtesy Pirelli HangarBicocca. Photo Lorenzo Palmeri; 98-99t AA/M Jourdan; 98b Società Trenno Ippodromi di San Siro; 100-101t AA/C Sawyer; 100bl AA/M Jourdan; 100br AA/A Mockford & N Bonetti; 101bl Murphy/Alamy Stock Photo; 101bc AA/C Sawyer; 101br AA/P Bennett; 102bl Freeartist/Alamy Stock Photo; 102br Freeartist/Alamy Stock Photo; 103t Digitalvision; 104t Brand X Pics; 105t AA/S McBride; 106t AA/M Jourdan; 108-112t AA/C Sawyer; 108tr AA/A Mockford & N Bonetti; 108tcr Stockbyte; 108cr Photodisc; 108br AA/C Sawyer; 114-125t AA/M Jourdan; 119cr AA/M Jourdan; 119br AA/M Jourdan; 122cr AA/M Jourdan; 124bl AA; 124br AA/M Jourdan; 125bl AA/P Bennett; 125br AA/C Sawyer

Titles in the Series

- Amsterdam
- Bangkok
- Barcelona
- Berlin
- Boston
- Brussels and Bruges
- Budapest
- Chicago
- Dubai
- Dublin
- Edinburgh
- Florence
- Hong Kong
- Istanbul
- Krakow
- Las Vegas
- Lisbon
- London
- Madrid
- Melbourne
- Milan
- Montréal
- Munich
- New York City
- Orlando
- Paris
- Rome
- San Francisco
- Seattle
- Shanghai
- Singapore
- Sydney
- Tokyo
- Toronto
- Venice
- Vienna
- Washington, D.C.